ʿReGENERATE

A GUIDE TO CONNECT GENERATIONS

So nice to meet you!
Jessica

JESSICA STOLLINGS

ISBN: 9781097513246

Published by Jessica Ink

Nashville, Tennessee

Dedicated to my mom and dad with heartfelt gratitude for teaching me what's important in life – and for always believing in me. It's an honor to further your legacy.

And to the five generations of family that have influenced my life, with respect for those who have come before and hope for those yet to come.

"Generations pass like the leaves fall from our family tree. Each season new life blossoms and grows, benefiting from the strength and experience of those who went before."

— Heidi Swapp

CONTENTS

PART II: CONNECT

How to bring different generations together, optimizing their collective strengths to improve outcomes

WHY GENERATIONS MATTER

Early in my research on generations, I conducted a series of video interviews to learn how growing up in different time periods impacts the way people see the world later in life.

As part of this project I interviewed my dad, a child of the 1960s, to capture his story and legacy for myself and my future family.

In Dad's typical style, he was all in.

I'll never forget the day he showed up at the studio in his best suit and a bright red tie. Before I knew it, these words came out of my mouth: "Perfect Baby Boomer look, Dad," I said. "You even wore a tie!"

In that moment, I watched my dad's powerful presence slump just a little bit. I didn't know why – until we got into our interview and he explained.

"Jessica, I would like to go back to the comment you greeted me with, the one about my suit," he said. "You see, I was very intentional about what I wore today. That intent was not to look a certain way or to play a part for your video. My intent was to honor you, because I believe in you and the work you are doing."

Now is the part where I re-live the sick feeling in my gut when I realized the very thing my dad sincerely did to honor me, I mocked.

Coming from a generation that often prefers flexibility over formality, I'd let my generational bias hinder me from seeing my own father in an accurate light.

Unfortunately, this happens all too often. Even with the best of intentions, many of our messages get lost in generational translation. And right now, with five generations bringing their unique perspectives into the workplace, the fallout of accumulated misunderstandings is wreaking havoc on all aspects of business – including morale, human resources, productivity, and the bottom line.

Consider these statistics: Age is the number one diversity issue in America.[1] More than a third of people waste five or more hours each week due to chronic, unaddressed generational conflict.[2] Turnover among Millennials – a generation currently in their 20s and 30s – is estimated at $30.5 billion each year.[3]

Tension between generations is nothing new; throughout human history, it has been necessary for each generation to forge a path between the ways of the past and the challenges of the future. What's new is the accelerated rate of change in our society – from technology disruption to communication trends to social norms. It's as if each generation has grown up in a different world, making misunderstanding all too easy and common.

A majority of companies report generational conflict, but only 20 percent have a plan to manage – much less optimize – these dynamics.[4] Buried in the frustration lies an untapped potential to differentiate yourself and your organization by bringing different generations together to understand each other, combine their diverse perspectives, and share knowledge to create innovative solutions to the complex challenges we all face.

The reality is that different generations still need each other – maybe now more than ever. We need young, raw talent and the energy and potential that it brings. We also need the wisdom and experiences of those who've lived more of life, who understand why a certain level of stability is needed to keep us all anchored.

Generations matter because each generation brings to the table a unique set of strengths that is important to our mutual success. Recognizing how different generations complement one another can help us move together into an increasingly positive future.

So, the question becomes: How do we do it? How do we bring perspectives together in ways that honor one another and drive better outcomes? And where do we start?

ReGenerate guides you through the steps you need to take to benefit from the generational diversity in your workforce.

Because in the midst of one of the greatest generational shifts in history, we have the opportunity to ask: What are we going to build, how can it be better, and how can we do it together?

Let's make it great.

Your friend,

Jessica

PART I: UNDERSTAND

How to relate to, communicate with, and empower each generation in the U.S. workforce

CHAPTER 1

UNDERSTAND GENERATIONS
A starting point

Generations are often classified based on their birth years. But more than just a demographic cohort, each generation has a distinct social or cultural identity influenced by large-scale trends and events that took place during its members' formative years.

Practically speaking, it's helpful to our everyday interactions – in the home, workplace, classroom, houses of worship, and communities – to have a basic understanding of these generational identities and how they shape people's expectations.

As with any other grouping of people in American society, a generation's worldview is influenced by a variety of factors – things like the economy, media messages, prevailing family structure, and major news events of their time.

As is true for people of different economic, geographic, or cultural backgrounds, groups of people who grow up in different eras often have different ideas about life and how the world should work.

THE AMERICAN MELTING POT

Imagine a group of strangers who've grown up in different parts of the country: a Wyoming rancher and a New England professor, a West Coast movie star and an Alabama factory worker, a first-generation Texan and a Florida retiree, a farm family from the Appalachian Mountains and one from the Midwest plains. Put them all in a room together and see how long it takes for a misunderstanding to occur.

In some cases, there may be a language barrier. Other differences might arise from things as simple as the landscape: How foreign do Nebraska's miles-long highways sound to someone who's never left the urban pavement? How can someone from the cool, wooded hills of West Virginia picture life in the hot Texan sun?

If you're in that room, it will help to understand the backgrounds of the people you're meeting with: their language, their landscape, their social and cultural influences, and how those things shape the way they see the world. These factors may explain why one person is worried about government interference while another calls for stronger policing, or why one is focused on the need for basic education and another on the pressure to meet fitness and fashion expectations.

THE GENERATIONAL MELTING POT

In our fast-changing American society, generational differences – the social and cultural influences that exist among people raised during different times in history – are every bit as distinct and as important in shaping how people interact with each other.

Imagine a group of strangers who've grown up in different times: a World War II veteran and a smartphone-connected tech worker, a free-love hippie and a 1950s housewife, a middle-class factory worker from the 1970s and an unemployed boomerang kid from the 2010s. Put a family from the penny-pinching Great Depression in a room with one from the consumption-driven 1990s, and see how the conversation goes.

Pretend for a moment that it's possible to put all of them together in a room at the same age. How can the wartime vet explain the value of his childhood outdoor play to the tech-savvy software designer who grew up playing video games with his friends online? How can the father of two who chose among plentiful factory jobs and bought a house at 25 make sense of why his single, debt-plagued counterpart would move back in with his parents at 26?

If you're in this room, it will help to understand the generations of the people there. This factor may help to explain why one person is worried about foreign policy while another is focused on neighborhood issues, or why one is focused on tax burdens and another on the burden of student debt. Even at the same age, they have different priorities that reflect what's going on in their time period.

In just a few short decades, Americans have gone from horse-drawn carriages to self-driving cars, from clunky telegraph wires that sent a few words in dots and dashes to pocket-size computers that can send a library of human knowledge across the globe with a tap on a screen or a word to a voice-activated AI.

As a result, social and cultural experiences vary from one American generation to the next in a way not experienced in most of human history.

SIMILARITIES, NOT STEREOTYPES

None of this is to say that members of a generation are all the same. Each person is uniquely made, and a wide variety of factors influence the people we turn out to be; there's no theory, tool, or test that can completely define who we are.

Studying generations is a little bit like observing trees in a forest: While each tree is different and unique, there are also similarities when they grow in similar soil, with similar conditions of rain and sunlight. Trees that grow in the open in deep valley soil will spread their limbs in a way that trees in a crowded forest do not. Trees on a rocky, high-elevation ridge will anchor themselves in crevices unimagined by those on flat ground.

It's possible to observe how different conditions influence the trees' way of living while also recognizing that not all trees in an area will grow exactly the same. That's also true of people: We can observe the influence of a cultural environment without making undue assumptions about people as individuals.

When researchers try to reduce people to stereotypes, it's referred to as "ethnographic dazzle" – a fancy word for being so enamored with surface differences that we miss important similarities. It's something that's important to avoid.

ReGenerate does not seek to create labels or stereotypes, but rather to shed light on the idea of generation as an important social and cultural influence that shapes individuals. Not everyone necessarily fits into the generation defined by their birth year, but everyone does identify, to some extent, with the defining experiences of a generation.

Whether the difference is location (place), generation (time), or any other behavior influencer, understanding why and how people approach situations differently can be a great help in resolving conflicts and creating win-win situations.

THE STUDY OF GENERATIONS

Generational theory, which seeks to explain how the era in which a person was born affects his or her development and worldview, is a relatively new social science. Though it has early roots in the 1920s, it was not popularized as a field of study until the 1990s.

According to generational theory, our value systems are shaped during the early years of our lives by our families, friends, communities, and – in our ever more interconnected world – media and defining national events.

In the 1920s and 1930s, the first serious generational scholar, Karl Mannheim, outlined the idea that each new generation experiences a gap between the ideals learned from older generations and their own experienced realities of life.

As a result, a generational consciousness is formed out of "a common location in the historical dimension of the social process."[5] The resulting mentality and defining values continue to influence individuals throughout their lives.

For example, many of those who experienced the Great Depression – an era that was just beginning as Mannheim penned his essays – went on to be financially prudent throughout their lives. And many of those who served in World War II never lost the sense of duty that was necessary to defeat Hitler.

It's important to also note that generational differences are not the same as life stage differences, which change as a person ages. A teenager is in a different life stage than a parent of young children, who is in a different life stage from someone whose children are grown and on their own.

Unsurprisingly, a person's priorities, responsibilities, and outlook shift as they move from one life stage to the next. That's a good thing: a sign of growth! Generational characteristics, however, are enduring, meaning they remain constant throughout all stages of life.

DEFINING SOCIAL AND CULTURAL GENERATIONS

In their book *Generations*, William Strauss and Neil Howe helped to popularize the idea that people in a particular age group tend to share a distinct set of beliefs, attitudes, values, and behaviors because they grow up and come of age during a particular period in history. They summed it up this way:

"History creates generations, and generations create history. The cycle draws forward energy from each generation's need to redefine the social role of each new phase of life it enters. And it draws circular energy from each generation's tendency to fill perceived gaps and to correct (indeed, overcorrect) the excesses of its elders."[6]

Strauss and Howe defined a "social generation" as the people born over roughly a 20-year span, about the length of one phase of life. More recently – particularly as the pace of technology development alters society on a much shorter timeline – researchers are looking at the possibility that, culturally, generational shifts are happening much faster, perhaps in half the time.

GENERATIONS ACROSS THE GLOBE

Just as each generation in the United States has grown up in a unique social and cultural time, other countries around the world have their own set of social, political, and economic factors that influence the identity of each generation.

The generational information in this book is specific to the U.S. workforce; we cannot apply it broadly across a global workforce. At the same time, the insights presented here on how to bring different generations together can also be useful tools to build effective working relationships among people with other differences.

Interestingly enough, we're seeing more convergence of trends in younger generations across the globe because they have exposure to many of the same international events. There's no question that as the world continues to become more connected, having the skills to bring together people of different backgrounds will only grow in importance.

Tammy Erickson and Timothy Blevins, thought leaders on global generational trends and the changing workplace, explained it well:

"As global business becomes the norm, companies that succeed at building and engaging a multigenerational, multi-geographical workforce will benefit enormously, in innovation and on the bottom line. With the increasing importance of talent as a competitive factor, the ability to recognize and capitalize on the significant differences in workforces around the world and across the generations is one of the most important strategic opportunities for decades to come."[7]

A QUICK GLANCE AT TODAY'S GENERATIONS

Most researchers recognize five generational identities that represent the experiences of those born during the last century. Here is a brief overview:

Generations at a Glance

BIRTH YEARS	A.K.A.	DEFINING MOMENTS	
TRADITIONALISTS			
1925-1945	"Silent Generation"	• Great Depression	• World War II
BABY BOOMERS			
1946-1964	"Boomers"	• JFK Assassination • Civil Rights • Vietnam • Moon Landing	• Sexual Revolution • American Dream
GENERATION X			
1965-1980	"Baby Busters" "Gen-Xers"	• Challenger Disaster • Berlin Wall	• Divorce • MTV • "Latchkey Kids"
MILLENNIALS			
1981-1996	"Echo Boomers" "Generation Y"	• 9/11 Attacks • School Shootings	• Y2K • Social Media
GENERATION Z			
1997-2012	"iGen" "Homelanders" "Screeners"	• Great Recession • First African American president	• Terrorism • Technology

The major events that impact each generation occur when they are adolescents and young adults. This youthful period of their lives is often when their worldviews and opinions form and can be influenced by trends and events.

For example, Traditionalists were shaped by World War II because many were of military age during the war. Baby Boomers were influenced by the Vietnam War and the Civil Rights struggle because many were teens and young adults at the time.

Gen-Xers were impacted by the rise in divorce because many of them saw their parents split up when they were kids. Millennials were influenced by the fear of school shootings and terrorism because many such incidents occurred during their education years. Generation Z has been influenced by social media-driven culture because smartphones became popular during their school years.

Though earlier generations have also been studied, this book will cover the five generations in the U.S. workforce today: Traditionalists, Baby Boomers, Generation X, Millennials, and Generation Z.

As we get to know these generations, please keep in mind that one generation is not "better" or "worse" than another; one should not be glorified while another is ignored. Every generation has unique strengths and challenges, and all of the generations complement one another.

The 1930s were the golden age of radio. In that era families gathered around their radios to hear news, sports, music, game shows, and dramatic stories.

CHAPTER 2

MEET THE TRADITIONALISTS

1925–1945 | 27 million of U.S. population | 2% of U.S. workforce

The Traditionalist generation experienced a lot in their early years. They lived through the Great Depression and World War II, two events that would shape the 20th century on a global scale. Their collective experience – from economic privation to wartime rationing – is one of making do and stretching a little bit to go a long way.

Growing up, family and faith were paramount to the Traditionalist generation. Sunday church, followed by a big lunch and time with extended family (who often lived close by), was a savored weekly tradition.

"When I was born, the United States was going through the Great Depression. My family was in a serious state of poverty. However, I never knew I was poor. I always had clothes. I never went to bed hungry. We always had plenty of food because my mother had a huge garden, and I think she planted everything but the kitchen sink!

What we did during my generation really helped lay the foundation for today's generation. I have that feeling because we paid the price. We made it. We survived in spite of all the handicaps; in spite of all the obstacles, we survived."

— Jewel, born in 1929

ABOUT THE TRADITIONALISTS

Traditionalists grew up in challenging times where loyalty to family and country and a self-sacrificing sense of duty were essential. Hard work was important, and most members of this generation were raised in traditional nuclear families where men earned the income and women took care of the home and children. The Traditionalists are also known as the "Silent Generation" for their propensity to adhere to accepted standards.

TRADITIONALIST TRENDS:

Their reality growing up: Hard times on the home front

Defining moments: Great Depression, World War II, Korean War

Where they went for information/entertainment: Radio

Their values: Loyalty, patriotism, duty before pleasure, faith, family, respect for authority, the common good

Who they admire: Presidents, generals

Their goal: Work hard and build a legacy (at work or in the home)

A typical "life path": Military service, early marriage and children, homemaking (women), working for a company for 30+ years and moving up over time (men), retirement with a pension, grandchildren

What they consider professional work attire: Suit and tie; skirt suit and hose for women (if and when women joined the workforce)

Communication style: Often modeled after the military chain of command. For example: "Here's what we're going to do; now, do it!"

Organizational style: Order, structure, and hierarchy

Learning style: Their education was one-way, strict, and structured. Their view of problem-solving in the workplace is often similar.

Strengths: Work ethic, loyalty, emotional maturity, stability, legacy, willingness to work together

Challenges: Reluctance to "buck the system" or make needed changes

In a word: Steady

OTHER THINGS TO KNOW ABOUT TRADITIONALISTS:

▸ For the most part, Traditionalists believe rules were made for a reason and should be followed rather than questioned.

▸ They like to partner with institutions for the greater good. For example, becoming involved in civic clubs was very common and respectable when they were younger, and many Traditionalists still comprise the membership in those clubs today.

▸ They tend to have conservative views of family, religion, and country.

▸ Their word is their bond. Traditionalists grew up in a time when handshakes were as legitimate as contracts.

TRADITIONALIST VIEWS ON:

Work: Work is an opportunity, and hard work will bring rewards over time.

Religion: Faith is foundational, and religious services should be attended every week.

Education: Education is a privilege.

Parenting: Children have a responsibility to help as part of the family, and they should generally be seen and not heard. Family meals are important.

TRADITIONALIST WISDOM:

"Rome wasn't built in a day."

"Waste not, want not."

"Save for a rainy day."

TRADITIONALISTS TODAY:

The Traditionalist culture is still alive in many longstanding organizations. Though their numbers in the workplace are declining, their thinking remains – and it can cause tension when the foundations they laid are disrupted.

Some companies are slowly reducing the time Traditionalists spend in their operational roles, leaving them time to transfer knowledge or to loan their skills to a nonprofit.

Traditionalists

Military Service: A Social Obligation

When they were young, men of the Traditionalist generation served in the armed forces in greater numbers than any generation since, in large part because of World War II. Many still consider military service to be an important and honorable duty.

PERCENTAGE OF MALE VETERANS BY GENERATION [8]

TRADITIONALIST MEN 24% **BABY BOOMER MEN** 13% **GENERATION X MEN** 6% **MILLENNIAL MEN** 2%

The Weekly Faithful

Traditionalists continue to attend church more than other generations. Many consider involvement in a faith community to be an important part of their participation in society.

PERCENTAGE OF EACH GENERATION WHO ATTENDED CHURCH WEEKLY IN 2014 [9]

TRADITIONALISTS	BABY BOOMERS	GEN X-ERS	MILLENNIALS
👤👤👤👤👤	👤👤👤👤	👤👤👤	👤👤👤
48% ATTENDED	37% ATTENDED	33% ATTENDED	30% ATTENDED

Life as a "Company Man"

Most Traditionalists have built successful careers through long-term employment, working 20 or more years for a single company. Younger generations, by contrast, have been accused of chronic job-hopping. According to Anya Kamenetz in *Fast Company*, the average length of time a person stays in his or her job is 4.4 years.

PERCENTAGE OF WORKERS AGE 35–64 IN THEIR CURRENT JOB FOR MORE THAN 10 YEARS [10]

1975	1980	1985	1990	1995	2000	2005	2010

💼 **51%**
>10 YEARS

💼 **39%**
>10 YEARS

WHEN RELATING TO TRADITIONALISTS, KNOW THAT THEY OFTEN THINK:

▸ Faith, family, and country are important.

▸ Traditional values should be upheld.

▸ It takes time and hard work to build a legacy.

▸ Hierarchy and structure help to keep order.

▸ Authority should be respected.

▸ There is a clear distinction between right and wrong.

TIPS TO CONNECT WITH A TRADITIONALIST:

▸ Spend time with them and ask about their lives and experiences.

▸ Respect authority and norms of courteous behavior.

▸ Use more formal communication in e-mail, such as proper capitalization and grammar.

▸ Be thoughtful about how you frame your "why" questions.

▸ Work hard and pay your dues.

▸ Help them capture their stories to share with emerging generations.

REFLECT:

▶ Who is someone you know from the Traditionalist generation?

▶ How does this person reflect and not reflect the generational trends?

▶ What strengths do this person and Traditionalists bring to your team and life?

▶ What is one thing you appreciate about the Traditionalist generation?

▶ What is one way you can connect with and honor a member of the Traditionalist generation?

The 1960s were the heyday of television. When families across America gathered for their evening programs, they could see real and fictional events unfold on their TV screens.

CHAPTER 3

MEET THE BABY BOOMERS

1946–1964 | 74 million of U.S. population | 25% of U.S. workforce

The Baby Boomers grew up in a time of economic prosperity and great change, and with the advent of television, they were able to see national and world events unfold daily on the evening news. Their collective experience – from the Cold War to the tumultuous Civil Rights struggle – was one of shared fear and excitement, a sense that times were changing and that they were part of momentous historical events.

Looking back at the big changes that took place during their youth, such as improved racial equality, sweeping social programs, and the moon landing, they remember the sense of hope that enabled them to feel like they could shape their own destiny in the midst of change.

"I remember seeing the Beatles on television on The Ed Sullivan Show. *They came in, played their guitars, and introduced a new style of music. I remember my dad's comments afterwards about how long their hair was, and I can't remember the words he used...but they weren't very complimentary.*

I also remember the excitement of hearing that we had actually landed on the moon.

Another early recollection is when John F. Kennedy was assassinated. It was like it was a continuous thing: John. F. Kennedy being assassinated, the Civil Rights movement becoming more visible and the conflict growing, and Bobby Kennedy being assassinated, who many people thought would be the next President of the United States, and of Martin Luther King Jr., certainly one of the greatest leaders of our generation, being assassinated...and then we moved straight from that into the Vietnam War."

– Mike, born in 1957

ABOUT THE BABY BOOMERS

Born during the spike in births that followed World War II, Baby Boomers grew up in a time of change on a national and global scale. Through events broadcast via television, they saw firsthand how individuals could make a positive difference in the midst of turmoil. When their sense of hope and possibility met the plentiful job opportunities of the booming postwar economy, the Baby Boomers found a path to economic prosperity.

BABY BOOMER TRENDS:

Their reality growing up: Big changes in American society

Defining moments: Moon landing, Civil Rights movement, John F. Kennedy assassination, Vietnam War, Watergate, Woodstock, feminist movement, hippie movement

Where they went for information/entertainment: Television

Their values: Ambition, hard work, pursuit of "The American Dream," potential for an individual to change the world

Who they admire: Leaders of social and cultural change

Their goal: Pursue the American Dream and live the good life

A typical "life path": Follow a certain path of work and/or education and receive the corresponding measures of success, including a happy family and ownership of a nice home and car

What they consider professional work attire: Business suit; in some cases, slacks and a collared shirt (men) or a skirt and blouse (women)

Communication style: Professional, face-to-face, phone, e-mail, politically correct

Organizational style: Structure, hierarchy

Learning style: In school, Baby Boomers were instructed by their teachers in a chronological fashion. They were trained to read a book page by page, from start to finish. As a result, Boomers often solve problems in a linear fashion, meaning A leads to B leads to C.

Strengths: Work ethic, dedication, optimism, competitiveness, structured thinking, knowledge and experience

Challenges: Difficulty with change

In a word: Ambition

OTHER THINGS TO KNOW ABOUT BABY BOOMERS:

▸ As young people, Boomers questioned authority much more than Traditionalists, and they encouraged equality. In many cases, they were free-spirited hippies before they came to the boardroom.

▸ More educated than previous generations, they were highly competitive when they joined the workforce. There are so many of them that they had to be.

▸ They are creative and savvy. The Baby Boomers sent a man to the moon with minimal technology and organized the Civil Rights movement long before the existence of social media.

BABY BOOMER VIEWS ON:

Work: Work hard, pay your dues, and move up the ladder. Dedication is a path to success.

Religion: Faith is important, and you should participate in religious services with your family.

Education: Education is valuable and leads to greater possibilities for your future.

Parenting: You should treat your children as individuals, encourage their uniqueness, maintain a close relationship with them, and provide experiences that you didn't have growing up.

BABY BOOMER WISDOM:

"Make love, not war."

"Civil disobedience works."

"Sacrifice leads to success."

BABY BOOMERS TODAY:

Baby Boomers are living longer, working longer, and reinventing what retirement looks like. In addition to sticking around in the workplace, many are launching "encore careers" as entrepreneurs. Even with Gen X and the influx of Millennials and Generation Z, the U.S. workforce as a whole is expected to continue growing older because hard-working Boomers aren't leaving.

Baby Boomers

Raised in a booming postwar economy, the Baby Boomer generation joined the workforce with high ambitions. They were able to achieve an unprecedented standard of living, with many measures of financial success increasing substantially.

U.S. HOUSEHOLD INCOME

$42,934	$46,842	$50,389	$52,784	$55,627
1967	1977	1987	1997	2007

Even adjusted for inflation, the median household income has risen steadily in the U.S. [11]

SIZE OF THE AMERICAN HOME

1,725 SQ FT	2,095 SQ FT	2,330 SQ FT	2,598 SQ FT
1983	1993	2003	2013

The average size of the American home has increased as Baby Boomers have increased their wealth. [12]

Who is Dr. Spock?

Dr. Benjamin Spock was a pediatrician whose writing influenced a shift in parenting attitudes in America. For half a century, his book *Baby and Child Care* was the second-best-selling book next to the Bible. Dr. Spock advocated that parents be more affectionate with their children and treat them as individuals.

In more recent decades, the attitudes he promoted have been blamed for creating young people who are less ready to face the realities of adult life. Parents who follow Dr. Spock's ideas have been accused of "self-esteem parenting" and "helicopter parenting."

Working Longer

According to the U.S. Bureau of Labor Statistics, about 40 percent of people ages 55 and older were working or actively looking for work in 2014. That number, known as a labor force participation rate, is expected to increase fastest for the oldest segments of the population – most notably, people ages 65 to 74 and 75 and older – through 2024. [13]

GROWTH RATE IN LABOR FORCE BY AGE (2014–2024 PROJECTION)

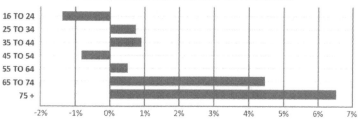

WHEN RELATING TO BABY BOOMERS, KNOW THAT THEY OFTEN THINK:

▸ If you work hard and do a good job, opportunities to progress should come; don't look for shortcuts.

▸ Having structure and a plan is a good thing.

▸ Long hours are sometimes necessary – and may be viewed as a measure of your work ethic.

▸ People should be recognized for their accomplishments.

▸ Leadership should be earned and honored, not questioned.

TIPS TO CONNECT WITH A BABY BOOMER:

▸ Respect their experiences and recognize their contributions.

▸ Take time to build rapport.

▸ Say "thank you."

▸ Use courteous, professional, structured communication.

▸ Ask them to lead and mentor.

▸ Continue to provide them with opportunities for learning and development, including reverse-mentoring from younger generations on topics like technology.

▸ Help Boomers capture and share their knowledge and ensure their legacy.

REFLECT:

▸ Who is someone you know from the Baby Boomer generation?

▸ How does this person reflect and not reflect the generational trends?

▸ What strengths do this person and Baby Boomers bring to your team and life?

▸ What is one thing you appreciate about the Baby Boomer generation?

▸ What is one way you can connect with and honor a member of the Baby Boomer generation?

The 1980s saw the growth of the personal computer. Now it was possible for an individual to access a vast array of information and work in a new way.

CHAPTER 4

MEET GENERATION X

1965–1980 | 66 million of U.S. population | 33% of U.S. workforce

Generation X grew up with the fallout of many of the social changes that began during the Baby Boomers' time. Among them: scandals in government and religious institutions, large-scale corporate downsizing that came with globalization, and changes to prevailing work and family structures – including mothers in the workforce, after-school "latchkey" care, and a high rate of divorce. This experience has left them with a more independent and skeptical approach to life, work, and family.

Generation X remembers the end of the Cold War, tragedies and successes in the space program, Operation Desert Storm, and the advent of personal computers, as well as the start of some troubling trends: the AIDS epidemic, the rise of crack cocaine, drunk driving, tainted Halloween candy, and the faces of missing children on milk cartons.

"I'll never forget the Challenger [space shuttle] disaster; everyone was watching it on TV at school because there was a teacher going into space and that was a big deal.

The other big thing was the coming down of the Berlin Wall. All those years of knowing the Berlin Wall had been there, then all of a sudden it was just being torn down by people my age and younger, which was pretty amazing.

I remember when they were making movies about my generation, like Reality Bites *and that kind of thing. We were called the slacker generation, which is such a misnomer. That's not what Generation X is at all. Flexible was the word that I had in my mind, and I think that's because things changed so quickly in our generation. We've had to be flexible, and so it's made us question when things don't change."*

– René, born in 1971

ABOUT GENERATION X

Gen-Xers grew up with an unprecedented pace of change, not only in the development of technology but also with the breakdown of major institutions, including the family. Also known as "Baby Busters," they are largely the children of Baby Boomers who intentionally had fewer kids than their parents did. Generation X was the first generation to experience 24-hour news coverage, personal computers, cable and satellite TV, video tapes, video games, fax machines, pagers, and cell phones.

GENERATION X TRENDS:

Their reality growing up: Change is constant in every aspect of life

Defining moments: Challenger disaster, Berlin Wall coming down, Operation Desert Storm, divorce, "latchkey kids," International Space station, HIV/AIDS epidemic, personal computers

Where they went for information/entertainment: Television and early Internet

Their values: Flexibility, work-life balance, skepticism, independence

Who they admire: Successful outside-the-box thinkers

Their goal: Enjoy life with a balanced approach; put family first

A typical "life path": Navigate a world of constant change, where the social and family structures their parents relied upon no longer exist

What they consider professional work attire: Business casual

Communication style: Relaxed, casual, e-mail

Organizational style: Decentralized and results-driven

Learning Style: Many Gen-Xers attended school in "pod" classrooms, where they had to learn to listen to the teacher while tuning out other noise. Their problem-solving and team-forming style tends to be integrated, often converging for a goal and diverging to solve independently.

Strengths: Adaptable, independent, flexible, creative, computer literate, productive, open-minded, not afraid to ask "why," work-life balance

Challenges: Reluctant to trust

In a word: Balance

OTHER THINGS TO KNOW ABOUT GENERATION X:

▶ Generation X, as a relatively small generation, sometimes feels left out and misunderstood.

▶ This independent, self-sufficient, skeptical generation is an expert at sniffing through a marketing ploy; to them, transparency is important.

▶ They're the last generation that routinely used handwritten notes and letters to communicate.

GENERATION X VIEWS ON:

Work: Work smarter, not harder. Employees should not be micromanaged; they should be given clear tasks and judged by results. Work can be done anywhere.

Religion: Faith is meaningful. Religion as an institution should be questioned.

Education: Education is a great opportunity and should be pursued. However, it's not a magic formula for success. You should be open to alternative paths.

Parenting: Family is first and foremost. Even when it's hard, you should be there for your child – and also give them room to mess up so they can learn and improve. Safety is important, and screen time should be balanced with the real world.

GENERATION X WISDOM:

"The only constant is change."

"You need work-life balance."

"Be skeptical first and build trust with time."

GENERATION X TODAY:

Gen X is sandwiched between the massively large Baby Boomer and Millennial generations. That can benefit them at work: Gen-Xers report being equally comfortable with technology as Millennials, and they also show a mastery of conventional leadership skills more on par with Baby Boomer leaders.

Generation X

'Til Divorce Do Us Part

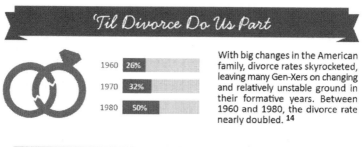

Year	Rate
1960	26%
1970	32%
1980	50%

With big changes in the American family, divorce rates skyrocketed, leaving many Gen-Xers on changing and relatively unstable ground in their formative years. Between 1960 and 1980, the divorce rate nearly doubled. [14]

"We're Here, Too!"

In the generational family, Gen X is the middle child. They are often overlooked and misunderstood. According to the DDI Global Leadership Forecast 2018, Gen X accounts for 51% of all global leaders, yet is the most passed-by for promotions and slowest to advance. With an average of 20 years of workplace experience and comfort with technology, they are primed to quickly assume nearly all top executive roles. [15]

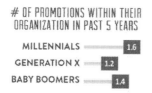

 # OF PROMOTIONS WITHIN THEIR ORGANIZATION IN PAST 5 YEARS

MILLENNIALS	1.6
GENERATION X	1.2
BABY BOOMERS	1.4

AVERAGE # OF DIRECT REPORTS

Gen X leaders have 7 direct reports on average
(2 more than Millennials, 1 fewer than Baby Boomers)

Seeking Work-Life Balance

With the large-scale corporate downsizing of the 1970s and 1980s, members of Generation X saw the pain inflicted on their parents. People who'd bought into the promise of 30 years and a pension got burned – and Gen-Xers vowed never to be them, instead pursuing more independent and flexible routes.

70%

Sylvia Ann Hewlett notes in the *Harvard Business Review* that 70% of Gen-Xers say they prefer to work independently. [16]

37%

Research by Hewlett and Lauren Chivee highlights another trend where 37% of Gen-Xers have "one foot out the door" of their current jobs, and they are looking to leave their current employers within three years. [17]

WHEN RELATING TO GENERATION X, KNOW THAT THEY OFTEN THINK:

- ▸ Personal or family life comes first before work, clubs, and other commitments.

- ▸ You should be skeptical first, trusting only when it's proven safe.

- ▸ It takes time to build trust, and transparency is the first step.

- ▸ It's important to ask and understand "why."

- ▸ Rules are just guidelines, and the status quo should be challenged.

- ▸ Balance and flexibility are key.

- ▸ You have to go with the flow.

TIPS TO CONNECT WITH A GEN-XER:

- ▸ Be open, honest, and transparent; know that it will take time to earn their trust.

- ▸ Promote work-life balance; reward with flexibility and mobility.

- ▸ Partner them with mentors they respect.

- ▸ Share a need, and then let Gen X figure it out independently.

- ▸ Give them space; do not micromanage.

- Show respect for their time, be efficient, and use results-based language.

- Empower Gen-Xers to be translators between Baby Boomers and Millennials.

- Give them opportunities for outside learning and coaching through virtual and traditional training.

BONUS TIP ON RELATING TO GENERATION X:

Embrace questions and use them to help you improve.

For Generation X and the generations that follow, asking "Why?" is not necessarily about challenging authority. While older generations may consider it irritating or even insubordinate, more recent generations view it as an important way of learning how the world works.

Gen-Xers, who grew up in a time of social and economic upheaval – and, in many cases, the breakup of their families – have a different outlook on the world than past generations. That skepticism that always asks "Why?" is tied to a search for deeper understanding.

When Gen-Xers ask "Why?" they're saying, "I care enough to ask" and "I'm interested" and "I want to know where I fit into the bigger picture so I can do a good job."

A willingness to embrace these questions and invite feedback is a way to create a workplace where people feel valued, appreciated, and part of a team working toward a meaningful goal.

REFLECT:

▸ Who is someone you know from Generation X?

▸ How does this person reflect and not reflect the generational trends?

▸ What strengths do this person and Generation X bring to your team and life?

▸ What is one thing you appreciate about Generation X?

▸ What is one way you can connect with and honor a member of Generation X?

By the late 1990s, laptops were common on college campuses. Built to accommodate life on the move, they transformed work and communication into something that could be done anywhere.

CHAPTER 5

MEET THE MILLENNIALS

1981–1996 | 71 million of U.S. population | 35% of U.S. workforce

Millennials were the first generation to grow up with personal computers as a part of life. Some older Millennials got their first computers in high school, while younger Millennials had them in the home since birth. Millennials grew up in an era of increasing diversity in the U.S. and increasing globalization and technology, shaping their interconnected perspective of the world.

In the instant-information age, Millennials are troubled by the violent trends of school shootings and terrorism that affect everyday people, and their perception of the world was shaped by the horror of the 9/11 attacks. Despite the fears generated by these events, Millennials as a group have a sense of optimism and a strong desire to make a positive difference in the world.

"9/11 was a really big, distinct moment that I will never forget, along with the ridiculous amount of violence within schools. I feel like every six months something crazy, like the Batman movie [theatre shooting], happens and it gives our age group a bad name.

I think technology has made us really aware and passionate to see change; you see a lot of people post on Facebook and different social media sites about injustices and violence. Those things aren't really left under the radar anymore; that's cool to see that people actually care about justice in this world right now.

Our generation can make a positive difference in violence, in areas like sex trafficking and modern-day slavery, and just so many different avenues of injustice that might not have been brought to light in years past just because of lack of information, lack of technology. To be able to have so many resources and outlets, I think it's spurring our generation to be more passionate and active."

– Trevor, born in 1992

ABOUT MILLENNIALS

Millennials, also known as "Echo Boomers" or "Generation Y," grew up in a world with a whole new dimension: technology as a means to interact with and exchange information. This explosion of technology has meant exposure to a wide range of worldviews, ideas, and cultures; it has also given them access to world events in real time and has provided them with an outlet to broadcast their thoughts as they happen. Technology has infiltrated every aspect of their lives, fundamentally changing the way this generation communicates and sees the world.

MILLENNIAL TRENDS:

Their reality growing up: Technology shapes the present and the future

Defining moments: 9/11 attacks, terrorism, Y2K, school shootings, reality TV, laptops, cell phones, online social networks

Where they went for information/entertainment: Internet

Their values: Creativity, collaboration, diversity, inclusion, authenticity, purpose, open-mindedness, entrepreneurialism, passion for global issues

Who they admire: Cause-oriented individuals and entrepreneurs

Their goal: Make a difference and change the world

A typical "life path": Pursue what they're passionate about and see where it leads; they are "dream job" chasers in search of their calling and ideal life

What they consider professional work attire: Anything that expresses their individual style

Communication style: Social media, texting, technology

Organizational style: Networked and relational; a team, not a hierarchy

Learning style: In school, they did projects in groups. It's no wonder they prefer to work and solve problems together in swarm-like clusters with leaders in the middle of the network. Millennial thinking and problem-solving is highly interconnected.

Strengths: Tech-savvy, well-educated, high performing, networkers, confident, creative/entrepreneurial, optimistic, diverse, civic-minded, willing to work hard to make a positive difference

Challenges: Sense of entitlement, short attention span, dependent on parents

In a word: Passion

OTHER THINGS TO KNOW ABOUT MILLENNIALS:

▸ They grew up multi-tasking: studying on their way to soccer practice while eating a fast-food burger.

▸ Though they're very cause-oriented and will readily support specific efforts or companies, they don't like to be branded with a religious or political category.

▸ Raised by younger Baby Boomers and older Gen X parents with a self-esteem focus, many of them have been sheltered, protected, praised, and privileged — and grew up with a paralyzing array of choices.

▸ They've experienced a major focus on safety, both in terms of crime/terrorism fears and in terms of parental supervision and strict regulations on everything from cribs and car seats.

▶ Most of them are burdened with student loan debt, and many have trouble finding work; however, they've largely faced the Great Recession with optimism.

▶ Millennials are growing up later, getting married later, and rethinking traditional "rites of passage" like home ownership. This is starkly different from past generations. Many demographers call this trend "emerging adulthood" to represent a new life phase between childhood and adulthood. [18]

▶ Millennials, who often live alone, register high rates of depression, anxiety, and loneliness.

▶ Millennials are a diverse generation. They were the most racially diverse generation in U.S. history until Generation Z emerged.

▶ Only 13 percent of Millennials say their career goal involves climbing the corporate ladder to become a CEO or president; by contrast, two-thirds say their goal involves starting their own business. [19]

MILLENNIAL VIEWS ON:

Work: Work should have meaning and align with your purpose, whether you work for yourself or for a company.

Religion: Ask questions rather than accept religion on blind faith. Participating in organized religion can help you gain spiritual community, but it's more important to put faith into action.

Education: Higher education is a good thing, but a pricey college degree might not help you as much as you thought.

Parenting: You should be "parent ready" for children, and you should nurture them. Dads should be involved, and everyone in the household should have a say. Crowdsourcing parenting advice is easy but can be overwhelming amid the Pinterest-perfect images and tips.

MILLENNIAL WISDOM:

"Follow your passion."

"Make a difference every day."

"Express yourself."

MILLENNIALS TODAY:

Millennials are the largest demographic group in the U.S. labor force, which will greatly influence the workplace. With immigration, Millennials are expected to keep growing in the population at large, surpassing Baby Boomers in 2019.[20]

Millennials

Majority of the Workforce

More than one-in-three American labor force participants (35%) are Millennials, making them the largest generation in the U.S. labor force, according to a Pew Research Center analysis of U.S. Census Bureau data. Their collective mindset is shaping the workplace of the future. [21]

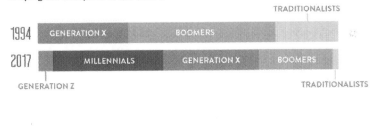

The Online Universe

SOCIAL MEDIA USE BY GENERATION [22]

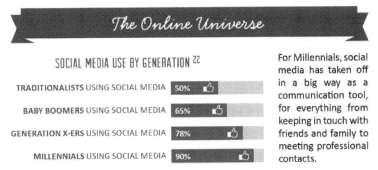

TRADITIONALISTS USING SOCIAL MEDIA 50%

BABY BOOMERS USING SOCIAL MEDIA 65%

GENERATION X-ERS USING SOCIAL MEDIA 78%

MILLENNIALS USING SOCIAL MEDIA 90%

For Millennials, social media has taken off in a big way as a communication tool, for everything from keeping in touch with friends and family to meeting professional contacts.

No Rush to the Altar

Millennials are getting married far less than past generations. Here's the percentage of Millennials who are married, compared with other generations when they were the same age (18-32) that Millennials are now. [23]

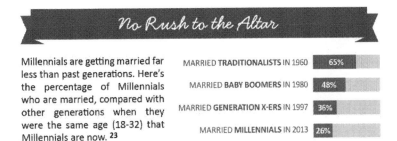

MARRIED TRADITIONALISTS IN 1960 65%

MARRIED BABY BOOMERS IN 1980 48%

MARRIED GENERATION X-ERS IN 1997 36%

MARRIED MILLENNIALS IN 2013 26%

WHEN RELATING TO MILLENNIALS, KNOW THAT THEY OFTEN THINK:

▸ It's easier to relate to family, friends, mentors, and coaches than to a "boss" figure.

▸ It's best to work together as a team.

▸ You can work remotely via technology; flexibility is key.

▸ Marriage, religion, and all traditional institutions/organizations are questionable.

▸ Life should be lived purposefully and in pursuit of the "ideal."

TIPS TO CONNECT WITH A MILLENNIAL:

▸ Communicate expectations from the start and offer ongoing, two-way feedback.

▸ Build genuine relationships; get to know them as people. Millennials are highly relational.

▸ Be transparent and authentic. Create a safe place for questions and doubts.

▸ Connect with a cause.

▸ Allow them to be creative and entrepreneurial.

▸ Provide mentoring, coaching, and teamwork; help them identify their strengths and where they fit in the bigger picture.

▸ Make sure you use the right communication channels. (Hint: don't call; text.)

BONUS TIPS ON COMMUNICATING WITH MILLENNIALS:

▸ Rather than creating new programs, communicate what you currently have that Millennials want. In other words, tell them "why" they should be interested in your organization. If you're not sure what will interest them, try this exercise:

Make a list of two columns.

In column 1, jot down your organization's mission, vision, values, and culture attributes. You can also list the programs, policies, and initiatives that are going well for you. In column 2, based on what you've learned about Millennials, make a list of what they are looking for in a job. Circle the areas of commonality and promote those opportunities first!

Here's a chart for you to practice.

OUR ORGANIZATION IS PROVIDING...	MILLENNIALS ARE SEEKING...

▸ Make your messages short and interactive with visuals, action words, and forward-looking phrases.

▸ Don't lecture. Instead, ask questions and foster a dialogue.

▸ Evaluate your visual presentation and consider that Millennials are more drawn to fonts that look handwritten, colors that are green and earthy, and videos that are raw and relaxed (think YouTube).

REFLECT:

▸ Who is someone you know from the Millennial generation?

▸ How does this person reflect and not reflect the generational trends?

▸ What strengths do this person and Millennials bring to your team and life?

▸ What is one thing you appreciate about the Millennial generation?

▸ What is one way you can connect with and honor a member of the Millennial generation?

The early 2000s brought ubiquitous smartphones, app-based commerce, and global social media. Suddenly, anyone – and everyone – could be a star.

CHAPTER 6

MEET GENERATION Z

1997–2012 | 73 million of U.S. population. | 5% of U.S. workforce

For a while the jury was out on what to call this generation, which is now entering the workforce. I used to call them iGen, but that was before the polls came in. "Gen Z" has won out as the most recognizable name, particularly when searched on Google.

Gen Z is coming of age in a post-9/11 America, where their personal news feeds have been filled with stories of terrorism, Twitter wars, #hashtag movements, and reminders of what to do if there's an active shooter in the classroom...or the movie theatre. They've experienced both the benefits and pitfalls of being constantly connected by technology – a reality they were born into – which has influenced how they interact, communicate, learn, and see the world.

The fallout of the Great Recession has influenced their practicality and their focus on stability, safety, and security. As the most diverse generation in history, one that grew up with the first African American president, they instinctively recognize the value of tolerance and inclusion.

"I don't feel like our generation has one defining moment. We have experienced the fallout of 9/11. Every day it seems like we hear about another act of terrorism or mass shooting. These events do not scare me, but they do make me aware of my surroundings at all times.

President Obama was elected when I was growing up, which was a milestone.

One of my favorite memories was when the iPad released! Growing up with smartphones and tablets has totally changed the way our generation learns and interacts socially. My parents taught me to be cautious with technology, to be careful what I post.

What bothers me most is the polarization of our country. We are so divided; it's like we can't find common ground on any issues. We fight about gun control and immigration and Democrat versus Republican labels. The only thing we can agree on is food. We all like to eat! Maybe we start rebuilding our relationships at the table?"

– Daniel, born in 2000

ABOUT GENERATION Z

Everything you can say about the impact of technology on the lives of Millennials can be multiplied many times over for Gen Z, which is the first generation of true digital natives; many of them have been using Internet-connected touchscreens since birth. By middle school much of their social life revolves around what happens online, and getting a smartphone is viewed as an important rite of passage. Isolation behind a computer screen has been linked to high rates of loneliness and depression.

GENERATION Z TRENDS:

Their reality growing up: Uncertain economic times, post-9/11 fear of terrorism, ubiquitous technology and social life primarily online

Defining moments: Great Recession, smartphones and tablets, first African American U.S. President, mass shootings, the War on Terror, same-sex marriage, online causes and movements, polarized U.S. politics. Some defining moments may still be unfolding.

Where they went for information/entertainment: Smartphone, social media platforms like YouTube, SnapChat, and Instagram

Their values: Practicality, equality, inclusion, innovation, integrated thinking, healthy and loving family

Who they admire: Social entrepreneurs and YouTube stars

Their goal: Work hard to fix root-level issues; change the broken system rather than engage in it

A typical "life path": Seek out education that makes sense, find a stable career path and stick with it while exploring various side hustles, possibly do several rounds of this over the course of a long life

What they consider professional work attire: Open to what the company requires and what fits their personal brand

Communication style: Technology-based, less words, more images. Face-to-face for important conversations, but short and to the point

Organizational style: Customized with a focus on connection, and integrated as needed: office and home, coffee shop and co-working spaces, virtual and in-person meetings

Learning style: Best as active participants in hands-on, experiential, and project-based learning – including opportunities to be involved in teaching

Strengths: Aware of society and self, hard-working, entrepreneurial, tech-savvy, open-minded, inventive, undeterred by complex challenges

Challenges: In-person communication, emotional intelligence, mental wellness

In a word: Practical

OTHER THINGS TO KNOW ABOUT GENERATION Z:

▸ They're on-demand consumers and used to instant access to information, communication, and online product delivery. They're comfortable with the shared economy; app-based ride-sharing, apartment-sharing, and rental clothing are part of the norm.

▸ Gen Z has grown up in a variety of changing and non-traditional family arrangements. To them, social trends like same-sex marriage, non-traditional gender roles, and ethnic diversity are simply part of life.

▶ The Great Recession hit their parents hard, so they know how to do without and work for things they want; their focus on work and their conservative outlook with money reflect this.

▶ They're questioning traditional models of education and are open to learning through school-industry partnerships with hands-on, experiential, and project-based learning, as well as through alternative routes like e-certificates and online tutorials.

GENERATION Z VIEWS ON:

Work: Work hard and seek job security, along with a personal brand and side hustle.

Religion: No, thanks. According to a Barna study, the percentage of Gen Z who identifies as atheist is double that of the U.S. population.[24]

Education: Education is important, but it must have a good return on investment.

Parenting: Be there for support and guidance, but kids need to learn how to function on their own and be resilient in a tough world.

GENERATION Z WISDOM:

"Practicality over passion."

"If you want something done right, do it yourself."

GENERATION Z TODAY:

Generation Z is entering the workplace differently than previous generations – for instance, they are not working summer jobs at the same rate and they are coming into the workforce later.

Generation Z

Gen Z is the first generation of "digital natives," meaning they've had widespread access to technology since birth; this has fundamentally changed the way they interact with the world, communicate, consume and create media, work and manage relationships.

U.S. ADULTS WITH ACCESS TO INTERNET [25]

1995   14%
2014   87%

SELFIES TAKEN EACH DAY BY PEOPLE AGES 18–24 [26]

1 MILLION

GEN Z-ERS WHO USE THEIR DIGITAL DEVICES IN BED [27]

91%

In for the Long Haul

Gen Z is hard-working, with a focus on long-term stability. While freelancers and side hustles are part of the norm, they're very interested in applying their entrepreneurial skill in a job. [28]

76%

76% of Gen Z is willing to start at the bottom

75%

75% of Gen Z is more worried about starting a career than finding a soulmate

61%

61% of Gen Z say they would stay at a company for 10+ years

Diversity is a Given

A Pew Research Center analysis of U.S. Census Bureau data finds that Gen Z is the most racially and ethnically diverse generation; only 52% of them are non-Hispanic whites. [29] And 77% of them say a company's level of diversity impacts their decision to work there. [30]

% SAYING INCREASING RACIAL AND ETHNIC DIVERSITY IS A GOOD THING FOR OUR SOCIETY [31]

GEN-ZERS	62%
MILLENNIALS	61%
GEN-XERS	52%
BABY BOOMERS	48%
TRADITIONALISTS	42%

WHEN RELATING TO GENERATION Z, KNOW THAT THEY OFTEN THINK:

▸ It's tough growing up in a world where everything is captured and curated online.

▸ Technology can improve the workforce and lead to innovative solutions.

▸ Time is better spent solving complex problems than propping up existing models. For example, find a better solution to hunger instead of volunteering at food banks.

▸ Important conversations should be held face-to-face.

▸ Whether in person or electronic, communication should be straight and to the point, and summed up with images when possible.

▸ Resources should be stewarded and shared.

▸ It's important to protect the environment.

TIPS TO CONNECT WITH A GEN-ZER:

▸ Be authentic and show genuine interest in getting to know them as people.

▸ Listen to their stories and empathize.

▸ Connect with them early in life, with a realistic and practical message tied to tangible outcomes – like how your company can help them build a stable career.

▸ Optimize technology with a relevant website and updated info/communication via digital tools.

- Customize everything and communicate in visual, digestible chunks.

- Partner as much as possible; bring together business, education, and community for real-world learning, projects, and impact.

- Embrace "Yes, and..." thinking – a job and a side hustle, learning and teaching, tech-based and face-to-face.

- Teach discernment and digital stewardship, which includes setting healthy boundaries with technology and looking beyond curated feeds of information.

REFLECT:

- Who is someone you know from Generation Z?

- How does this person reflect and not reflect the generational trends?

- What strengths do this person and Generation Z bring to your team and life?

- What is one thing you appreciate about Generation Z?

- What is one way you can connect with and honor a member of Generation Z?

CHAPTER 7

LEARN MORE ABOUT GENERATION Z

Newest generation in the workforce

As Gen Z has begun to shake up the classroom and enter the workforce, I've received a lot of questions about what to expect – and it seems I'm not alone. A Ford Motor Company study found the majority of adults believe kids today have more in common with their global peers than adults in their own country![32]

So, I wanted to share a little more on America's newest rising generation.

With much of this generation still in its formative years, some of the trends are still forming. At the same time, there's a lot we already know.

On the technology front they have a lot in common with the generation preceding them. Like Millennials they are tech-savvy, with a communication style rooted in technology. But in other ways – including their outlook on jobs and the workplace – they're very different from Millennials.

So far, researchers have identified three major influencers that have impacted the worldview of Gen Z: growing up with touchscreens in hand, being the most diverse generation in history, and experiencing the Great Recession.

PINPOINTING TRENDS

Generational researchers put the start of Gen Z around 1997 and the end around 2012. The reasons have a lot to do with the trends and events that have shaped American society during this time frame.

For example, the year 2007 – about the time the oldest members of Gen Z were preparing to enter middle school – is considered an important turning point in technology. That was the year Apple launched the iPhone, Facebook and Twitter went global, Kindle and Android were released, Airbnb was founded, Google bought YouTube, and IBM created its artificial intelligence system, Watson.[33]

But these trends are only part of the story. According to generational theory, a generation's mindset is also influenced by how it fits into the broader generational cycle. As the theory goes, all of the generations living at a particular time complement one another by providing a full set of the traits, strengths, and experiences needed by society.

In this case, a lot of parallels have been drawn between Gen Z and their great-grandparents' generation, the Traditionalists.

A generation impacted by the Great Depression and World War II, the Traditionalists played an important role in building the infrastructure and institutions we have today. Known for a sense of duty, patriotism, a strong work ethic, and commitment to the common good, the Traditionalists sought to solve society's challenges by building things like hospitals, roads, businesses, charities, and government safety net programs.

Gen Z does seem to have some similarities to the Traditionalists. For example, the Great Recession may be to Gen Z what the Great Depression was to the Traditionalists in terms of forming a practical outlook focused on work and stability, as well as their responsibility with money and resilience to challenges.

The War on Terror may be to Gen Z what World War II was to the Traditionalists, forever shaping their view on the lack of security in the world and the need to work together on common problems. Like the Traditionalists, Gen Z has a clear interest in building society and solving global issues – with proposed solutions that, similarly, involve top-down action, such as centralized efforts by government.

Interestingly enough, both of these generations have come of age at a time referred to by researchers as a "fourth turning" – a stage at which the generational cycle begins its repeat. This is considered a significant time of social upheaval and societal change, and some predict that Gen Z will spearhead changes of significant magnitude, just as their great-grandparents did.

FIRST DIGITAL NATIVES

You're at the gym for an exercise class, and you can't help but notice, in the corner, several small children looking at little screens while their moms work out. One of them, barely seven, is watching YouTube videos on her mom's phone.

That moment could be an illustration of Gen Z's relationship with technology: They may have been more proficient with the Internet as toddlers than your parents ever became in their lifetime. In some ways this is a good thing – for example, inventive use of tech could help create a more efficient, effective, and innovative workplace – but in other ways, it's devastating.

The social significance of growing up with Internet-connected touchscreens cannot be overstated. The kinds of outdoor play and in-person interaction that were once considered critical to a child's development have been almost completely replaced with interaction on digital devices.

Picture a gorgeous Saturday – blue sky, sun shining, 70 degrees, and a light breeze. The subdivision streets are empty. The kids are inside: playing games on their phones, messaging their friends, and checking social media. Their social reality is driven not by the gorgeous weather outside, but by what other kids post online.

Naturally, technology has influenced the way this generation sees the world, interacts with others, communicates, learns, creates, solves problems, and consumes media. And there's a pernicious downside: as social media and texting have replaced #IRL (in real life) activity, there's been a major jump in anxiety and depression. Life satisfaction rates have dropped. Loneliness is on the rise. Unfortunately, so is suicide.[34]

After reviewing decades of data, psychologist and researcher Jean Twenge put it this way: "iGen [Gen Z] is on the verge of the most severe mental health crisis for young people in decades." She attributes one of the root causes of this alarming trend to the rise of smartphones.[35]

Part of the problem is the "always on" nature of the devices – and the social expectation that people will be "always on" too. Gen Z is so used to having their phones with them all the time that they report major distress when separated from their devices.

For the most part, past generations could experience the predictable drama of middle and high school and then come home to other things – family life, or perhaps interaction with neighbors. Gen Z, by contrast, has faced constant social pressure to stay connected through messaging in the evening and during the weekend.

All that screen time also creates a bit of a distorted perception that encourages them to compare the average moments of their own lives against the most showcase-worthy moments of others' lives — a seemingly perfect online picture of others' parties, purchases, and perceived popularity.

For those with Millennial parents, it doesn't help that they've also grown up with some pressure at home to take great selfies and appear to be a Pinterest-perfect family.

Interestingly enough, some Gen-Zers have mobilized technology in efforts to improve upon the social isolation it can create. For example, at one school a Gen-Zer started a movement called #WeDineTogether to ensure that no one would get stuck eating alone.

Gen Z knows how to optimize technology to achieve outcomes and promote causes, and their understanding of the world is influenced by hashtag social media movements — for example #BlackLivesMatter, #BlueLivesMatter, #PrayForParis, and #MeToo.

There's reason to hope that Gen Z will continue to adapt ways to use technology to bring people together — even as it seems to separate them.

THE MOST DIVERSE GENERATION IN HISTORY

In reflection of major demographic trends, Gen Z is the most diverse generation in American history; according to the Pew Research Center, only about half (52%) of this generation is made up of non-Hispanic whites.

As a result, Gen Z has been culturally influenced by the growth of several ethnic groups. Gen Z has a much larger percentage of people of Hispanic or Asian cultural origin. The percentage of immigrants, meanwhile, is similar to that of past generations.[36]

To Gen Z, diversity is a core value, as are ideas like fairness and equality. Diversity, to Gen Z, is not an issue that requires education or awareness; it's who they are. They have an inherent understanding that people of very diverse backgrounds can work together well and create good outcomes together.

Beyond racial and ethnic makeup, Gen Z has also experienced more diversity in social aspects of life than past generations.

For example, they've been brought up in a variety of changing and non-traditional family arrangements. To them, societal shifts like same-sex marriage and non-traditional gender roles don't come with the negative associations these may have had for past generations.

Many view equality on issues like marriage and gender identity to be civil rights issues, much the way crusading Baby Boomers viewed working toward racial equality as important during the Civil Rights struggle of the 1960s.

The ethnic and social diversity of Gen Z presents a challenge to organizations, which must learn how to communicate clearly across a sea of differences. It also presents a remarkable opportunity to tap into the talent of a diverse group of people who are used to working together with people of widely varied backgrounds.

CHILDREN OF THE GREAT RECESSION

Members of Gen Z are being raised by Gen X and Millennial parents, and the Great Recession hit their parents hard. They know what it is to do without and work for things they want — and their focus on work and financial responsibility reflect that.

The fallout of the recession has impacted them in a surprising number of ways, affecting everything from their view of work to their approach to education.

Though they may not be entering the workforce as early as their older counterparts did, when they do so they come ready to start at the bottom and work hard over time. According to survey data, nearly two-thirds say they would stay at a company for more than

10 years – and of those, nearly a third would be willing to stay for more than 20 years.[37]

Even with an array of options in todays' high-tech economy, Gen Z remains focused on long-term stability.

Most of them also show up with a personal brand and a side hustle (think selling on Etsy, driving for Uber, or freelancing in various forms), a staple of income-earning power in a challenging economy. The side hustle is the equivalent, for many, of earlier generations' summer jobs. Companies that recognize this "side hustle" mentality as an asset – and integrate an entrepreneurial, freelance-like culture – will attract and engage Gen Z.

Gen Z's desire for safety and security also spans beyond finances; research shows that, compared to previous generations, Gen Z high school seniors are less likely to speed, drink alcohol, and have sex.[38] Safe spaces – environments that shield individuals from criticism and physical or emotional harm – are emerging at colleges and in the workplace. Teens are less likely to go out without their parents or even get a driver's license. When they do buy cars, their vehicle decisions are based on safety and affordability over brand.[39]

Another way the Great Recession has impacted Gen Z is in the way it's causing them to question the traditional model of education. After watching their Millennial elders struggle with student loan debt for degrees that did not provide employment, some wonder whether a college degree is worth the investment – especially since a large percentage of jobs they'll be eligible for likely don't exist yet.

They value higher education, and a large percentage are attending college, but they're also open to alternative routes of learning like online courses, e-certificates, and YouTube tutorials.

They're also open to learning through school-industry partnerships – and those partnerships are working, especially with hands-on, experiential, and project-based learning styles that enable middle and high school students to apply their creativity and solve real-world problems.

While some companies are starting to take recruiting cues from online dating apps, which use artificial intelligence to match potential job candidates with potential roles, others are connecting with Gen Z by offering hands-on education programs that are designed to develop a pipeline of future employees.

GEN Z VS. MILLENNIALS

This is a question I hear a lot: Are Gen-Zers like Millennials, or are they different?

In some ways, Gen-Zers are like Millennials on steroids: Millennials are diverse, educated, and comfortable with technology; Gen Z is all those things, only more so.

Millennial and Gen Z thinking is reshaping the workforce, and these generations seem to agree on much of the overall direction. They're on the same page about things like integrating technology and training workers to use it, providing remote working opportunities, hiring freelancers, and prioritizing the future.

But there are also important differences between Millennials and Gen Z.

For example, Millennials largely grew up in the self-esteem movement and in prosperous economic times, which left them with an optimistic bent. Gen Z, raised largely by skeptical Gen-Xers in a tougher economy, tend to see the world through a more pragmatic lens.

While both generations tend to have good relationships with their parents, the way they interact with them is different. When Millennials text their parents about a difficulty, their parents — largely Baby Boomers — are likely to swoop in to help their kids fix the problem. That's what got them the nickname "helicopter parents." When Gen-Zers text their Gen-Xer parents with a problem, they're more likely to be told lovingly to apply their intellect and figure it out on their own.

Work motivators and styles also diverge between these two generations. Millennials are primarily passion-driven, seeking meaning and purpose in their jobs. Gen-Zers, by contrast, seek a more practical purpose: a steady paycheck and visible career path.

Millennials tend to be more collaborative, seeking to work together. Gen-Zers, by contrast, are much more independent – and they don't seek the same level of collaboration. Gen-Zers also tend to be a lot more private than Millennials, choosing not to over-share their weekend misadventures with bosses and co-workers.

While Millennials have gained a reputation for job-hopping often, Gen-Zers generally seek to stay at a company longer. And while Millennials often seek to move up the ladder quickly, Gen-Zers have a greater willingness to stick around and pay their dues – assuming the reward is clear.

CHAPTER 8

SEE DIFFERENTLY

Examples of generational insights in action

By now you probably have a pretty good idea which generation you belong to, based on your birth year or the social and cultural events you remember. It's also possible that you were born "on the cusp" between two generations – meaning that, because of where you fall on the time-cultural continuum, you could identify with characteristics of two generations.

A common example are those people, like me, who were born in the late 1970s and early 1980s. "Xennials" is a term that's gained momentum to define this group of "cuspers" who grew up playing Oregon Trail, a very basic computer game about life on the frontier, when they were in grade school.

Regardless of the generation you identify with, the same rules for interaction apply: understand your own outlook and make an effort to understand other perspectives.

The model for learning generational competency is much like for emotional intelligence or EQ:

▸ Understand your own generational perspectives

- ▸ Manage your own generational perspectives

- ▸ Understand other generational perspectives

- ▸ Manage relations with other generations accordingly

CAN YOU REMIND ME WHY ALL THIS MATTERS?

Great question! I wrestled with it for years. Even a few years after launching my business full-time, I was unsure of the transformation that generational insights provided for my clients.

I'll never forget a year-end meeting with my mentor when I communicated the struggle of not knowing my value proposition. I shared a survey I'd crafted in hope that clients would share feedback on my purpose, but nothing compelling came through.

My mentor, in his wisdom, said: "You forgot to ask the most important question."

"What?" I said. I had spent hours on the survey. "What question did I miss?"

"What job did your clients hire you to do?" he asked.

"To speak on how to harmonize the generations...?" I said.

"Are you sure?" he asked, "Or is that just what you think they want?"

I reached back out to my clients, with one more question: "What job did you hire me to do?"

Their feedback, to my surprise, had a consistent theme — and it had nothing to do with generational harmony: "We hired you to help us see differently...to open our eyes...to challenge our paradigm." It was then I realized that all along I'd been in the perspective-shifting business.

That day, in talking out my findings with my mentor, my vocational purpose statement was born: I share insights and shift perspectives, inspire connections, and optimize the strengths of all generations to build a flourishing future.

GREAT, BUT HOW DOES THIS WORK IN REAL LIFE?

Embracing generational diversity can help us reduce conflict and strengthen our relationships, both personally and within organizations. By understanding other generational viewpoints — and how they relate to your own — you can interact with greater understanding and ultimately better results. Here are some example scenarios that clients have shared.

SCENARIO 1: PUSHY OR PROTECTIVE?

A Millennial was walking at an indoor track when she passed a Traditionalist man who yelled, "You are going the wrong way!" To her, his approach felt a little harsh.

Old views: What is his problem? Why is he yelling at me? What a grumpy old man!

New views: Perhaps he's trying to caution me about a danger in the communication style his generation is used to, which is very direct.

Results: The man later came up to the young lady to check on her; he'd seen someone going the wrong way on the track get injured a few weeks before. "Glad you're ok," he said. "Have a great day!"

SCENARIO 2: RUDE OR RESPECTFUL?

Two Millennials were pitching a research concept to a Gen-Xer to see if her firm would be interested in partnering on the study. Three lines into the pitch the Gen-Xer said, "Nope. This is not a fit for us. I don't want to waste anyone's time! Best wishes on your project."

Old views: She was so rude to cut us off! She could have at least heard us out.

New views: Gen-Xers are straight shooters and value efficiency. Perhaps it was because she respected us that she did not waste our time and freed us to direct our energy elsewhere.

Results: Within minutes of the conversation, the Gen-Xer sent an email about what a cool project it was, copied to a firm for whom it might be a better fit. That firm ended up being a major partner of the study.

SCENARIO 3: PENSION OR PAYBACK?

A Baby Boomer in HR was working on an updated benefit strategy to better accommodate a shrinking workforce profile and budget cuts. She was really stuck on how to make the company attractive for Millennials entering the workforce.

Old views: We have to figure out how to keep funding retirement and other traditional benefits to attract young workers.

New views: Millennials are buried in student loan debt; maybe help with student loan payback would mean more to them than money for retirement – and it's cheaper for us! Millennials also sometimes struggle with what they call "adulting."

Results: The company rolled out a new benefit to help employees pay down student loan debt and offered adulting classes. This saved money and motivated Millennials to stick around. The company's recruitment and retention rates went up.

SCENARIO 4: REJECTION OR REGARD?

A Millennial woman was managing a Baby Boomer man. Their team was moving into a new building that had both offices and cubicles. She excitedly showed the Boomer his new office, because she thought that was important to his generation. He did not accept it.

Old views: Here I was trying to do something kind, and it was met with rejection. Go figure; he probably just doesn't like change.

New views: This kind of behavior seems out of character. Perhaps there is a generational issue at play, and I should ask him about his motivation.

Results: The Boomer employee didn't feel his rank warranted an office larger than the one used by his boss. Out of respect for her leadership, he wanted her to have it. He rejected it because he wanted better for her.

SCENARIO 5: HATEFUL OR HELPFUL?

A Baby Boomer e-mails a Gen-X worker: "You need to get this report in immediately."

Old views: What a demanding statement.

New views: Maybe he's trying to help by being direct about the urgency of this project.

Results: Once he had the report in hand, the Baby Boomer went on to "sponsor" the Gen-Xer's work project, getting it out in front of the executive team.

SCENARIO 6: DISCONNECTED OR DILIGENT?

A Gen-Zer was looking at his phone during a meeting with the team. His Traditionalist boss was furious.

Old views: This worker is not listening or being present in our meeting.

New views: Perhaps he's actually looking up the things I'm talking about or using the phone for work reasons.

Results: During the meeting, the boss was asking for ideas to honor a board member. By the time the meeting was over, he had four concepts in his inbox from the Gen-Zer. In addition, all of the team action items the leader asked him to tackle were in motion. The Gen-Z worker had done it in real time.

FROM FRICTION TO OPPORTUNITY

Generational disconnects can be avoided through education and awareness. It's important to approach generational issues with an open mind about other perspectives, seeking — as Stephen Covey advocates — to understand first and to be understood second.[40]

Conflict reduction, productivity increases, collaboration, unity, engagement, retention, and innovation are just some of the returns on investment you'll get from using a generational lens. I can't tell you how many emails I've received after keynotes that underline this message: "You saved my employee's job!" "This mended my relationship." "I think we can now fix our recruiting problem."

The goal is not for anyone to be "right" or "wrong," but to understand one another and reach creative resolutions that result in a smoother-functioning workplace or organization – one that gets better and stronger with time.

KEY TAKEAWAYS FROM PART I

Part I of this book is the first step toward bridging generational gaps by understanding one another. It's important not to stop the conversation there, however. Part II contains the "how to" steps that will take you from this initial understanding to a well-functioning, generationally diverse workforce. Here are the key takeaways from Part I.

▸ When we study generations, we look at the social and cultural influences that impact a group of people as they come of age.

▸ Generational trends are similar to, but different than, life stage trends. In each decade of life, our priorities shift and change;

this is natural and a sign of growth. Generational influences are enduring and follow us throughout all life stages.

▶ Learning about generations is not about stereotyping, but about understanding. Each one of us is unique and different, and it's simply one of many lenses that can help us relate better with others.

▶ There are five generations represented in the U.S. workforce today: Traditionalists (1925–1945), Baby Boomers (1946–1964), Generation X (1965–1980), Millennials (1981–1996), and Generation Z (1997–2012). Check out the chart on the next few pages for a snapshot of core trends!

▶ Over the past 50 years, a lot has changed in U.S. culture. Technology disruption is a major contributor to societal shifts, but it's not the only factor. We've also seen a growing detachment from traditional institutions like political parties, religion, the military, and marriage. Meanwhile, the racial and ethnic makeup of the country has changed, college attainment has risen, and women have greatly increased participation in the workforce.[41]

▶ We're in the middle of one of the greatest generational and cultural shifts in our history. Along with globalization, technology disruption, and the fast-moving complexity of modern society, we're living in what generational theorists call a "fourth turning" – a time when institutions are torn down and rebuilt from the ground up.

▸ We have the opportunity to honor the legacy of those who've come before and walk with them through change while we equip and empower emerging generations for success. Together, we can build something even stronger and more enduring.

REFLECT:

▸ What is one thing you see differently after reading Part I?

▸ How will you apply what you've learned?

▸ Assess yourself. Based on your answers below, what is one thing you can do to boost your generational competency?

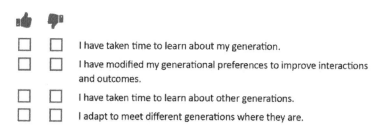

👍	👎	
☐	☐	I have taken time to learn about my generation.
☐	☐	I have modified my generational preferences to improve interactions and outcomes.
☐	☐	I have taken time to learn about other generations.
☐	☐	I adapt to meet different generations where they are.

MOVE FROM INSIGHTS TO ACTION:

▶ Observe generational interactions and see if you learn anything from them.

▶ Make an intentional effort to share a smile or to say "hello" to someone from a different generation.

▶ Think about small ways you can communicate better with members of other generations.

Generation Overviews

	TRADITIONALISTS	BABY BOOMERS	GENERATION X
BIRTH YEARS	1925-1945	1946-1964	1965-1980
A.K.A.	"Silent Generation"	"Boomers"	"Baby Busters" "Gen-Xers"
DEFINING MOMENTS	• Great Depression • World War II • Korean War	• JFK Assassination • Civil Rights • Vietnam • Sexual Revolution • Moon Landing • Watergate • Woodstock	• Challenger Disaster • MTV • "Latchkey Kids" • Berlin Wall • Divorce • Space Station • Operation Desert Storm
CHARACTERISTICS	• Loyal • Patriotic • Duty before pleasure • Respect authority • Build a legacy	• Hard-working • Dedicated • Ambitious • Optimistic • Competitive • Sacrifice for success	• Independent • Skeptical • Balanced • Flexible • Mobile • Life, then work • Ask "why?"
CONNECTION POINTS	• Ask about their lives • Respect authority and norms of courteous behavior • Work hard and pay your dues	• Respect their experiences • Recognize their contributions • Take time to build rapport • Utilize their knowledge	• Embrace their questions • Earn their trust • Be open, honest, and transparent • Promote life-work balance

MILLENNIALS	GENERATION Z
1981-1996	1997-2012
"Echo Boomers" "Generation Y"	"iGen" "Homelanders" "Screeners"
• 9/11 Attacks • Y2K • School Shootings • Reality TV • Technology • Social Media	• Great Recession • First African American president • Terrorism • Mass shootings • Political division • Technology • "Internet famous"
• Tech-savvy • Multi-taskers • Well-educated • Collaborative • Creative • Passionate • Global • Civic-minded • Diverse	• Diverse • Digital natives • Practical • Hard-working • Fiscally conservative • Equality minded • Socially conscious • Entrepreneurial
• Communicate expectations from the start • Offer feedback • Provide mentoring, coaching, and teamwork • Promote your purpose	• Use technology • Offer hands-on learning • "Chunk" communications • Use more visuals, less words ☺ • Connect work and education • Be inclusive • Customize experiences • Optimize shared economy

PART II: CONNECT

How to bring different generations together, optimizing their collective strengths to improve outcomes

CHAPTER 9

SEVEN STEPS TO REGENERATE
A blueprint to benefit from generational diversity

When I founded my speaking company, ReGenerations, more than a decade ago, the concept of "generations in the workplace" was just starting to emerge as a topic of curiosity.

Most of my work, including my first book, focused on increasing awareness of the fact that growing up in different time periods can influence perspectives and that, without the right understanding, the clash of those perspectives can cause conflict that hinders personal and organizational success.

People were intrigued, and I witnessed a lot of "Aha! This makes so much sense!" light-bulb moments. But, like most things in life, the call for change didn't hit until the pain set in. That pain became real as my generation, the Millennials, entered the work force *en masse* to the beat of a different drum.

My phone, calendar, and frequent flyer miles blew up.

Since then, a lot has changed. Most Traditionalists have exited the workforce, and Gen Z has begun to enter. Baby Boomers are working longer; Gen X is stepping into a large percentage of leadership roles; and the largest generation in the workforce, the Millennials, are — how do I say this? — not so young anymore.

There's growing research on generational diversity, and people understand it more. In fact, a level of generational fatigue has set in. Most speakers and books on the topic just focus on generational differences, simply highlighting gaps that divide us rather than proposing solutions to bring us together.

People recognize now that generational issues are a thing, and what they really want to know is what to do about it. I wrote this book because there's a lack of resources on how to move from general comprehension to a culture of inclusion and innovation.

While I don't have all the answers, I have spent the past four years rolling up my sleeves with clients to figure this out. How do we move beyond silos and combine diverse perspectives? How can we benefit from generational diversity? Where do we start? How do we make it simple?

The steps I've developed through this process are designed to bring generations together in ways that honor and empower all perspectives to create breakthroughs and new paradigms.

In Part II, I will walk you through seven steps to ReGenerate your organization:

▸ Understand – Teach generations as a cultural competency

▸ Appreciate – Transform generational conflict into opportunity

▸ Communicate – Translate your message so everyone can understand

▸ Cultivate – Design a culture where all generations thrive

▸ Coach – Develop a framework for feedback

▸ Adapt – Apply a generational lens to forecast the future

▸ Share – Develop a process to transfer knowledge

Simply put, this is a guide for next steps and solutions, the "how to" of building generational competency, connection, and knowledge-sharing that will improve your workplace from generation to generation.

CHAPTER 10

STEP 1: UNDERSTAND

Teach generations as a cultural competency

THE CUBICLE FORT

I couldn't have asked for a more classic generational conflict than the one experienced by my very first client. The company had two employees working side by side – a Baby Boomer and a Millennial – who were driving each other mad.

Each day, the Boomer came early and stayed late. She refrained from checking personal messages during working hours and always prepared in advance for the next day's work. The Millennial, by contrast, rolled into the office around 8:00ish and packed up to leave before 5:00. She texted constantly, checked Facebook between meetings, and handled any evening work issues from home.

The Boomer felt like the Millennial was lazy, uncommitted, and disrespectful of company time; the Millennial, meanwhile, couldn't understand why her colleague was so uptight. When their frustration peaked, they came up with a solution. The company added a wall – a real physical barrier – between their desks.

A little bit of investigation revealed that the two employees had similar productivity levels, and their customers were pleased with their service. They both produced high-quality work; they just did it in very different ways.

The conflict had to do with their views of "hard work." To the Boomer, "hard work" was associated with time. To the Millennial, it was all about an outcome. Both of these views make complete sense, based on the workplace norms of the eras the employees grew up in.

Helping the company to work through this conflict resulted in a new understanding between the two employees.

It also revealed that many others in their workforce were building walls between generations, so the company decided to host awareness workshops. Out of these learning sessions, a cross-generational think tank was born to discuss generational dynamics and company goals – and how they might set up expectations and policies that are a win-win for everyone.

The Bottom Line: Without the right understanding, generational differences can lead to wall-building.

The Solution: The barriers that divide us fall when understanding rises. It's important to teach generations as a cultural competency: the ability to understand, communicate, and interact with others from different generations. Here are some ideas on how to do it.

1. PROVIDE EDUCATION ABOUT GENERATIONS

Consider hosting a speaker, training session, or education series about generations. Focus on the unique experiences of each generation and allow members of each generation to teach their segment in a fun and creative way. Sharing stories, memories, and lessons learned is always a great way to get the conversation started.

Here are some ideas that have been tried successfully:

▸ In conjunction with a speaking and training event, a company hosted a learning and development conference called "Looking Back, Leading Forward" with music from every decade. Participants dressed in the iconic fashion of their day and showcased the technology they used early in their careers.

▸ A church group hosted a cross-generational panel discussion on life, relationships, and faith across the generations. It was fascinating to see how many different views emerged from the different times and circumstances in which the panel contributors grew up. For example, a snippet on "dating":

▸ **Baby Boomer:** "Do you mean courting? My dad was very involved in the process."

▸ **Gen-Xer:** "We would go on dates to the mall: hanging out, watching movies, or playing in the arcade."

▸ **Millennial:** "Guys text me and want to come hang out, but I've never actually been asked on a date."

▸ **Gen Z:** "I swipe right or left, but it's rare that I actually meet them in person."

▸ A middle school asked students to interview and report on different generations within their families. The students were amazed to learn that their grandparents got married young, used party-line telephones, and organized major social movements without a hashtag.

2. MOVE FROM GENERATIONAL DIVERSITY TO INCLUSION

We often talk about how to reach a certain generation, but that generation is not represented in the room. Or we learn about different generations but don't take steps to bring them together. Inclusion – bringing people of all ages and stages together – is the next step.

▸ Include a variety of ages on your boards, hiring panels, leadership teams, and committees. Expect a learning curve for younger members and treat mistakes along the way as opportunities for coaching and mentoring.

▸ Organize cross-generational project teams to solve complex problems. An interesting starting discussion would be: "How could our company best reward employees for their contributions?"

▸ Mix up your community outreach groups. For example, you might pair a youth organization with a senior group for activities or service projects.

▸ Spend intentional time with family members (holidays are a great time to do this) by asking about their lives and experiences. It's your legacy you're learning about, too!

TRY THIS TOOL: GENERATIONAL HOMETOWN STORY-SHARING SESSIONS

If you're more than one generation apart, then your "generational hometown" so to speak – the cultural context in which your generation was raised – is likely very different. Pair up with someone from a different generation and choose a couple of the questions below to spark your conversation:

▸ What was life like for you growing up?

▸ What was happening in the world?

▸ What was the national mood or political environment?

▸ What was going on in education and psychology movements?

▸ How did you find out what was going on? Newspaper? Radio? TV? Online?

▸ How did you communicate with family and friends?

▸ What technology did you use?

▸ What were family structures like?

▸ What were the cultural "norms" of the decade you grew up in?

▸ What TV shows, movies, music, art, or books were popular?

▸ What was dating like?

▸ What did you do for fun? What were your hobbies?

▸ What was on your childhood Christmas list?

▸ What is your favorite tradition or memory from childhood?

REFLECT:

▸ Do you think the times you grew up in have influenced your expectations or views today? If so, in what ways?

▸ How could growing up in another time period result in different expectations or views?

▸ How could a generational lens help you be more effective in your work?

CHANGE STARTS WITHIN

Be willing to put on a generational lens to see the meaning behind different ways of doing things.

The Baby Boomer may be coming in early because she's competitive and links sacrifice with success; the Gen-Xer may ask you questions because he wants to improve an outcome for you; the Millennial may be texting all the time because it's her primary channel of communication for business contacts; the Gen-Zer may be working a side hustle because they're thinking about long-term sustainability.

When someone says or does something that irritates you, pause and ask yourself why. Could there be a generational difference at play? Think this through before you respond.

Once you understand some of the attitudes, values, and perspectives of other generations, adapt your style to meet them where they are. Whether that means adding "yes, sir" to a verbal response or texting your employee instead of calling her, you may be surprised at how far a small step of respect can go.

Be willing to think outside the box. My client's experience with the "cubicle fort" is evidence that people with very different generational styles can be equally good, productive employees. Can you offer the kind of flexibility in your organization that allows everyone to perform at their best?

CHAPTER 11

STEP 2: APPRECIATE

Transform generational conflict into opportunity

NEIGHBORHOOD WAILING

In my family we make a point to support one another – so when my sister Emily and her family moved a few years ago, my parents pitched in to help. After a long day's work, they were exhausted and ready for a well-deserved night's sleep.

That's when the noise started: a loud and unusual wailing. It sounded like a dog, but no one was quite sure what it was. It went on all night long.

The next morning a tired and frustrated neighbor came to ask my family if they'd heard the noise, hoping my sister's dog was not the source. It was natural to wonder what kind of family would be irresponsible enough to let their pet keep the entire block awake.

A little investigation revealed that the noise was from a neighborhood dog, whose name was Ally.

Ally's best buddy and sidekick of 10 years had passed away, and Ally was grieving. The wailing was the only way she knew how to express her heartache, pain, and loss.

Suddenly, everyone's perspectives shifted from judgement to empathy. And instead of finger-pointing, they offered love and support.

GENERATIONAL WAILING

How often do we judge each other with outward "wailing"? I've done it, and it's been done to me. In the world of generational relations, I see it daily. The noises sound something like this:

"What's up with their lack of work ethic?" | *"Why do they stay in the office so much?"*

"Why do they question me? Don't they respect my authority?" | *"Why do they shut down all my ideas?"*

"That's not how we did it." | *"Bust out of the mold!"*

Do any of these examples sound familiar? Much like the situation with Ally, it's all too easy to jump to conclusions without assessing the backstory: the "why's" behind each generation's perspective and the "how's" for bringing them together for better outcomes.

The Bottom Line: Though our initial reaction to a situation may be negative, it's important to understand all perspectives before we rush to judgment and react.

The Solution: To interact wisely and successfully we must develop generational fluency, which is the ability to recognize and adapt to the needs of multiple generations and leverage their collective strengths for the benefit of all. Practicing generational fluency involves using a four-step process – pause, filter check, step back, and adapt – to move from friction to opportunity.

GENERATIONAL FLUENCY

Understanding perspectives is important because what we think influences what we feel, and how we feel influences how we behave. Left unchecked, we can get caught in vicious cycles where we see others in a negative light – even when it's not warranted.

When we choose to view someone negatively, our actions follow. The other person picks up on our vibes and, often out of defense, puts up a wall that reinforces our already negative views of them. And then the negative cycles repeat.

To get out of this mess, one person must shift to a virtuous cycle, or a positive lens for thinking about others. When we choose to view someone positively, our actions follow. The other person picks up on it and removes their walls. And then there's space for engagement.

When confronted with a generational difference that rubs you the wrong way, consider these four generational fluency steps to transform your frustration into appreciation.

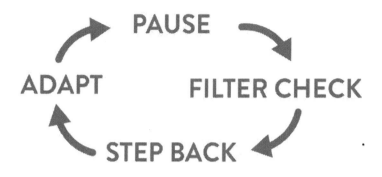

1. PAUSE: *Think before reacting or responding.*

Is the person you're interacting with a different age than you? If so, could there be a generational misunderstanding?

Take a deep breath when you want to react and give yourself the brain space to evaluate what's really going on below the surface. Beware of reacting when emotions are hot, as "fight or flight" communication never ends well.

Often, the issue of disagreement is the visual tip of a much deeper iceberg. Before you react, ask yourself questions like "Why does this bother me so much?" Asking "why" five times is one model for identifying a root cause.[42]

2. FILTER CHECK: *Consider how your generational experiences shape your views.*

How did the era you grew up in — the times, messages, media, values, and events — impact your perspectives today? Where did you get your views on workplace start times, communication norms, or dress codes?

Is your generational preference or "filter" hindering you from seeing younger or older co-workers in a positive light?

Explore your paradigm, or lens, for seeing the world. A lot of things have gone into the construction of your filter, from past experiences to personal insecurities. Think of this assessment like getting an eye exam to keep your vision or prescription up to date; it needs to be checked from time to time.

Sometimes you'll find no issues; other times, you might find your views are a bit fuzzy. It's also possible to have blind spots, so ask a trusted friend for feedback on your filter.

In this process it's also important to check for bias, which is favor for or against a thing, person, or group. Bias, often based on characteristics like age, weight, skin color, gender, religion, race, social class, ability or disability, sexual orientation, and even height, can be unconscious or conscious.

Left unchecked, bias tends to filter the information we collect, supporting our already held points of view and disproving points of view with which we disagree. It can lead to stereotyping about people of other generations in unfair ways, resulting in wrong conclusions and actions.

The truth is we all have biases. What are yours? Self-examination is critical, and the best way to bust a negative bias is to hang out with people who are different from you and get to know them as people.

Filter checking is not easy. It takes courage, but you can do it. Be brave!

3. STEP BACK: *Consider how different generational experiences shape others' views.*

Have you ever attended the same meeting as someone else and walked out with totally different perceptions of the experience? I recently went to a leadership conference with two friends, one a Baby Boomer and one a Traditionalist. Discussing it at lunch, we had vastly different impressions of the event:

> **Traditionalist:** *"That conference was over the top. I couldn't even understand the message with all the fanfare."*

Baby Boomer: *"What a great conference! Spot on!"*

Me (Millennial): *"I'm underwhelmed. I was expecting more experiential learning and interaction, especially from a conference that advocates innovation!"*

Each of us came with a frame. We talked about why we saw it the way we did, and from a generational standpoint it made total sense.

In everyday situations you can ask yourself: Why is your younger or older co-worker's approach frustrating you? Is it bad or wrong, or is it just different and reflective of the era in which they grew up? Are you taking time to listen and ask questions?

To understand someone's "why," remember to ask and not assume.

You can also try perspective-taking, which is the practice of considering alternative views of the same situation. Perspective-taking requires imagination, empathy, and asking others to help us see what we might be missing.

Sometimes you might step back and see that the other person is right, or you are right, or you're both right. As in this illustration, "right" often comes from where you're standing.

Credit: eDeliberation

In his book *Driven by Difference*, author David Livermore sums up the "stepping back" process like this:

"Culturally intelligent innovation begins with changing our impulse from *Why can't you see it like I do?* to *Help me see what I might be missing!* Together, we can each transcend and include our individual perspectives and upbringings to see the world more fully. We can work together to come up with the innovation solutions to solve problems big and small."[43]

4. ADAPT: *Combine your diverse views for a win-win.*

When we pause, filter check, and step back, we are then ready to adapt – to meet people where they are and fuse our perspectives for better outcomes.

If your perspectives are similar, how can you build on commonalities for success? If your perspectives differ, how can you work together in a way that gets results while respecting all points of view? When viewpoints are locked, ask: Is there a higher way that can transcend our individual thinking to create better realties? These are important questions to ask.

Sometimes the bridge-building process is easy; studies show that different generations have a lot more in common than they think. For example, in the workplace all generations are seeking meaning, appreciation, and flexibility; they just express these values in different ways.[44] Often, commonalities emerge that organically provide strong foundations for connection.

If similarities do not emerge, consider facilitating ways to find them. For example, one exercise is to put intergenerational groups together and ask them to find one thing that they all have in common, outside of the obvious things like working on the same team.

Sometimes combining differences is a bit more challenging and requires a mindset shift from "this *or* that" thinking to "this *and* that" thinking.

For example, author Malcomb Gladwell noted that older generations typically understand how workplaces and social organizations function in terms of hierarchy, while Millennials often see the world in terms of flat networks.

"What we need," Gladwell said, "is a system where we bring out the best of networks and combine them with the best of hierarchies."[45]

In moments when two mindsets are locked and unwilling to change, it's important to consider author Stephen R. Covey's explanation. In any conflict, Covey says the 1st Alternative is "my" way, and the 2nd Alternative is "your" way. The usual outcomes from this are continued divisiveness or compromise. Compromise stops the fight, but without breaking through to new results. A 3rd Alternative is that kind of breakthrough.[46]

It comes by asking if we can do better, defining what success looks like, imagining what third alternatives exist, and then arriving at synergy – a place of transformation.[47]

CASE STUDY: NESTERLY AS A THIRD ALTERNATIVE

Many elders want to age in place, but it's expensive, and they often need help with simple tasks — things like checking the mail, letting the dog out, running errands, and having help if a need arises. Their life stage can feel lonely, and they wonder where they fit.

Many young adults are graduating college buried in student loan debt, starting entry-level jobs with low salaries and wondering how they're going to pay their bills. Suddenly, their community of friends is scattered — and they often feel lonely, and they too wonder where they fit.

Nesterly is an online platform that seeks to tackle the challenges of housing affordability and aging in place with a simple solution: intergenerational home-sharing. You could think of it like an Airbnb of intergenerational living, making it easy for households to share an extra room with a young person.

Nesterly moves beyond singular issues, solving the challenge of home help and companionship for elders, affordable living and companionship for young adults, and retention of residents for communities. It's a win-win-win. Ultimately, this type of thinking will help us transcend our individual challenges and create new realities that benefit all.

TRY THIS TOOL: GENERATIONAL FLUENCY

Next time someone at work rubs you the wrong way, use these four steps to navigate the situation successfully:

1. Pause

▶ Is the person that is frustrating you older or younger? Could the issue be generational?

▶ Why is the situation bothering you so much? Have you asked yourself at least five times?

▶ Are you ready to respond respectfully, or are your emotions too high?

2. Filter check

▶ Why are you seeing the situation the way you are?

▶ What in your background might influence your perspective?

▶ Are any paradigm blockers or biases impeding your views of the situation?

3. Step back

▶ Could there be another way of seeing the same situation?

▶ What might impact the other person's perspective?

▶ Is the alternate view wrong, or is it just different?

4. Adapt

▸ What do you and the other person have in common? Could you start the bridge-building there?

▸ Is "yes, and…" thinking – combining both perspectives – a possibility in your situation?

▸ Are you willing to use "third alternative" thinking to create a new reality?

GENERATIONAL FLUENCY FOR YOUR ORGANIZATION

Pause, filter check, step back, and adapt is also a simple framework that teams can use and discuss at the institutional level. Questions like these can lead to new ideas and innovations:

Pause. The workplace is changing quickly. Is our organization reactionary, or ready for the shifts? Discern the times and consider how you might position your mission for success.

Filter check. What are our organizational norms? Are they still relevant? Are our leadership practices, culture, and systems helping or hindering our ability to see clearly and make wise decisions? Are we planning for the workforce of tomorrow through the lens of today? Take time to check your organizational vision for accuracy.

Step back. If we were our competitor, how would we outsmart our strategy? If we were our next generation of employees, what might we be seeking in employment? How do people outside of our organization perceive us and why? Consider how others might view your organization and what it means for how you continuously improve.

Adapt. In what ways do we need to change in order to ensure a thriving future? What are three ideas we can try in order to ensure relevancy and sustainability?

As you frame your questions make sure to position your challenge and opportunity in the same sentence. For example: How can we grow our company in the midst of Millennial turnover? Answering these hard questions with three words, "we can if..." challenges traditional thinking. It may take several lines of "we can if..." thinking to reach a breakthrough. It will be worth it when you do!

REFLECT:

▸ Are you hearing any "generational noise" or friction in the workplace? If so, why do you think it's happening?

▸ What's one way you can help diffuse conflict across generations?

▸ What's one way you can help utilize generational friction to produce innovation?

MOVE FROM WAILING TO WINNING

In honor of Ally, my challenge for you is to pause, filter check, step back, and adapt. To assume less and to understand more. To consider your own and others' views. And to adapt to meet people where they are – regardless of the noise.

CHAPTER 12

STEP 3: COMMUNICATE

Translate your message so everyone can understand

THE MOON WALK

At a recent training, I asked participants to share the first historical moment they remember. A Baby Boomer raised her hand and said, "The moon walk." Before she could finish describing this epic moment in history, a really excited 30-something responded, "The moon walk? I love that dance!"

Neil Armstrong and Michael Jackson both knew a thing or two about the moon walk!

To one generation, the phrase "moon walk" signifies an actual walk on the moon – an epic achievement of science and hard work. To another, it signifies an entertainer's signature move. Sometimes the words and phrases we use can have different meaning depending on the times we grew up in.

And then there's the diverse mix of channels we use to communicate with one another. Some generations prefer face-to-face communication, while others would rather email, text, snap, or slack. I've worked with many clients who were sending their messages via Facebook when their target audience was on Instagram.

Among a myriad of meanings, styles, and channels, how do we clear up the communication lines so everyone can hear and understand?

The Bottom Line: There's no one-size-fits-all approach to communication.

The Solution: Clarify the words you use and find out what channels are best for team members individually and as a group. Bring a cross-generational team together to determine how they can communicate with one another and which channels they'll be expected to monitor. Keep it simple.

1. BE AWARE OF WHAT YOU'RE NOT SAYING

Much of the time, how we are perceived by one another is based on our non-verbal communication, also known as body language, and the tone of our voice.

Non-verbal communication can send both negative and positive messages to others.

For example, if someone rolls their eyes or leans back and crosses their arms when you meet with them, this might send a message to you that they are frustrated. Poor posture and limited eye contact might signal insecurity, distractedness, or even lying.

Conversely, good posture, solid eye contact, firm handshakes, and leaning in towards others shows interest, confidence, and presence. Positioning your feet and body towards the other person shows you are "with" them.

Removing physical barriers that separate people can also go a long way. If you are meeting in your office, pull your chair out from behind your desk and place it by the person you are meeting with.

Being fully present, actively listening, and nodding your head to affirm the other person also demonstrates value.

If in doubt, smile. This widely accepted gesture of kindness sets a gracious tone.

Small, outward non-verbal tweaks not only create a welcome presence for others, they can also transform the way you feel on the inside, too.

2. USE UNIVERSAL COMMUNICATION STRATEGIES

While different generations often have different styles and channels of communication, there are other aspects of communication that are universal – meaning they apply regardless of one's background.

Here are some examples of ways to communicate that resonate with everyone:

▸ Share stories. Storytelling is a medium that unites us all as humans.

▸ Ask questions as they allow each person to relate the issue to his or her personal experience.

▸ Use facts – research and figures can open up a dialogue.

▸ Clarify, in vivid detail, exactly what you're talking about.

▸ Keep your language simple and avoid using slang or jargon.

▸ Stick to one topic at a time; cover one thing before moving on to the next.

▸ Break communication into "chunks," sharing step-by-step processes and needs.

▸ Support verbal communication with visual aids.

▸ Allow time for feedback and actively solicit it. When needed, have the other person repeat back what they heard.

▸ Be present. Be aware of your body language as well as the other person's.

▸ Listen more than you speak.

▸ Use multi-generational faces in your advertising.

▸ Use a variety of channels for your message, including newsletters, in-person meetings, e-mail, and social media.

▸ Create classic, timeless brands.

3. MAKE SURE YOUR MESSAGE IS RECEIVED

What's the best way to get in touch with the person you're trying to reach? To find out, ask them! If needed, adapt your style to use the platform they're familiar with. That might mean you text updates to your Gen Z workers, even though you still make a weekly phone call to your mother.

Stay balanced, keep an open mind, and don't expect one generation to suffer a major inconvenience to accommodate another. Each generation must be willing to adapt and collaborate, but it's your responsibility as the sender of the message to communicate your information in ways that will be received – even if that means using different channels to reach different people.

In addition to a channel for official messages, it's also important to have a channel where ongoing communication can occur. Be sure to choose a relevant channel for collaboration – whether that's e-mail, group text messaging, or social media – and make it clear from the start that everyone is expected to monitor and use this channel to stay in the communication loop.

4. CONSIDER THIS GENERATIONAL COMMUNICATION CHEAT SHEET WHEN RELATING TO DIFFERENT GENERATIONS

When communicating with Traditionalists and Baby Boomers, remember to:

▸ Use proper grammar and punctuation in written communications.

▸ Use courteous phrases like "Please" and "Thank you."

▸ Use respectful phrasing when asking "why" by first sharing your intent.

▸ Keep communications linear; step-by-step bullets are a great way to do it.

When communicating with Gen-Xers, Millennials, and Gen Z, remember to:

▸ Be open, honest, and transparent.

▸ Share "why" you are suggesting that they do something.

▸ Remain open for questions and two-way dialogue.

▸ Keep your messages short, visual, and to the point.

This chart can help you practice identifying your target audience and the channels, messages, and images that might engage them.

AUDIENCE	COMMUNICATION CHANNELS	MESSAGES THAT RESONATE	VISUAL SUPPORT
TRADITIONALISTS			
BABY BOOMERS			
GENERATION X			
MILLENNIALS			
GENERATION Z			
ALL GENERATIONS			

TRY THIS TOOL: TEAM TALK

Maybe your preferred method of communication is e-mail while your boss, who is 15 years older, makes phone calls more often and your newest teammates, who are younger, prefer to text.

Among a wide array of communication channels, it can be confusing to determine which to use for what purpose or person. There's not a right or wrong answer, but rather a set of questions like these, which can be talked out as a team:

- What primary communication channel do you prefer?

- What communication channel(s) work best for our team/project dynamics?

- Should we use different channels for short updates than for longer explanations?

- What channels are relevant for our team culture and context?

- In today's changing world, what communication approaches work best?

- Where can each of us adapt personally?

Bringing an intergenerational team together to hash out these questions is a great way to find solutions. It could also provide an opportunity to host a mentoring or reverse-mentoring "lunch and learn" on past and emerging communication forms. Often people don't want to use a channel simply because they're not familiar with how it works — and that's easy to fix because it only takes a few minutes to show them how!

Whatever mix you decide on, set clear expectations: "This is how our team is going to talk." Then, monitor feedback to ensure the outcomes are a win-win.

REFLECT:

▸ Have you observed or experienced a generational miscommunication? How was it handled? How could it be handled more effectively in the future?

▸ Who is responsible for ensuring that a communication is clearly received: the sender, the receiver, or both?

▸ In trying to reach multiple generations, should you use multiple channels? If so, how do you functionally manage multiple media?

▸ How do you know when you need to adapt to a communication channel that you aren't familiar or comfortable with? How do you know when you need to challenge the expectations or mindset of "This is how we've always done it"?

▸ What's one strategy you can use to ensure that your message is heard and understood by all generations?

FROM FUZZY TO CLEAR

Put in the hard work up front to determine your strategy and execution plan for effective communication. Know your audiences, the channels they use, and the messages that resonate with them. It'll take a little time to succeed across a sea of differences.

The clients I've seen do this well usually create one source of communication and then chunk it out across multiple media to reach their audiences.

For example, they might send an email with five bullet points. They do a "five steps how to" YouTube video with the same points. Then, they break down each of the bullet points by sending one out on Instagram daily with a supporting visual or text reminder.

Effective communication is not easy; there are many barriers to success. Your hard work up front will pay dividends with time in reduced conflict, questions, and miscommunications.

CHAPTER 13

STEP 4: CULTIVATE

Design a culture where all generations thrive

AN OFFENDING HAT

A recent training session with the leadership of a church camp resulted in a major breakthrough between two camp leaders, a Traditionalist and a Millennial.

Near the start of the summer, when the Traditionalist led the campers in the blessing of a meal, the Millennial unknowingly violated a rule of etiquette by keeping his hat on, an action the Traditionalist took as a major sign of irreverence.

In front of everyone, the older leader had scolded the younger, humiliating him in front of his peers and the campers.

As it turned out, the younger man had meant no disrespect; he'd simply never been taught that he was supposed to remove his hat during a prayer.

In our meeting, the Traditionalist wound up offering him one of the most genuine and heartfelt apologies I've ever heard. He'd assumed that the custom was universally known and hadn't realized his younger colleague was unaware.

Then, the Millennial broke down in tears. In addition to the hurt the incident had caused him, it had exposed a deeper insecurity: He wore the hat to hide the fact that he was losing his hair.

Once they talked through it, the Traditionalist resolved to try and avoid assumptions that would shame his colleague for things he may not know. The Millennial agreed to make an effort to show respect in ways that were important to the Traditionalist, even if he didn't always understand why. Healing occurred in the room that day, and it was powerful to watch.

The Bottom Line: Don't assume other generations know the same things you do. More often than not, they're starting from a different premise.

The Solution: Set clear expectations, communicate them often, and together build a culture conducive for diversity of thought and experience.

1. COMMUNICATE WORKPLACE NORMS CLEARLY

If your workplace has specific expectations, make sure you share them early on. For example:

▸ What time should employees show up, and what time should they leave? When you say 8:00 a.m., does that mean it's OK to show up at that time, or is your expectation that your team should arrive at 7:45 and be working by 8:00?

▶ Do you have a dress code? If so, what is it? If business casual, explain and show examples of what that means.

▶ Can employees text during office hours? Is it OK for them to use emojis with clients?

▶ Can employees work from home, and under what circumstances?

2. USE AN "ONBOARDING" PROCESS

Whether you're an established or emerging leader, spend time up front setting clear expectations and then checking in with the new members of the organization periodically to see how things are going.

Think of "onboarding" – the process of bringing a new employee on board – less as a one-day orientation and more as a months-long process of assimilation. This is also a great way to transfer your mission, vision, and values.

3. REVIEW WORKPLACE NORMS FOR RELEVANCE

As the world continues to change, it's worth pausing to consider what's going well and what can be improved within your organization. Which traditions, policies, and practices are driving value and should be continued? Which ones have been continued merely because they're comfortable? For example:

▸ Does it make sense to ban texting when it's a good way for employees to reach clients?

▸ Are you spending money on travel for meetings that could be handled by videoconference?

▸ Are you losing potential new talent by requiring suits and ties?

▸ Will allowing employees to work remotely save you space and money?

▸ Would a flexible schedule be as effective for some employees as working 8 to 5?

This kind of review is also a perfect opportunity to build understanding by bringing together a cross-generational team to work on the answers. It takes courage to work through these questions and make necessary changes, but in the long run your employees – and your bottom line – will thank you.

TRY THIS TOOL: DESIGN AN INTERGENERATIONAL CULTURE

All of these issues are important to think about and decide on together. Ultimately, they have to have leadership support. Then you have to ready the soil: the culture.

If the culture doesn't support generational diversity, then your efforts can do more damage than good.

For example, if you have a policy that allows workers to work remotely two days a week, but your culture doesn't support it, then there's often judgement when workers use their days. This creates friction from a policy that's meant to benefit everyone.

So, how do we create an environment for all people to thrive? To help us figure it out, I called on my good friend Tony Moore, the "culture architect." He shared these four steps, which can also be found in his book, *Culture in 4D*:[48]

1. Dream it. Bring together an age-diverse group of people and ask them what attributes must be present to cultivate a workplace culture and community where all people can belong and be successful.

For this step, have each person make a list of 3–5 specific words and phrases that answer this question – and then share why they came up with each word or phrase. Then, have the group refine the list together to their collective 3–5 characteristics that are most important for creating and sustaining an intergenerational culture. Typically, themes will emerge. These statements will help with this step:

▸ For all generations to thrive, the culture must be:

▸ Our top themes are:

2. Design it. Now that you've identified your collective top 3–5 themes, create very specific rules of engagement: Define what each theme means and how it is demonstrated behaviorally.

For example, if your team said "flexibility" is an important value for intergenerational success, clearly define what "flexibility" means for your shared relationship and how you will live it out with one another.

What behaviors demonstrate flexibility in the day-to-day work of your team? Working from home a few days a week? Leaving early to get to a child's soccer game? Pivoting midway on a project? Shifting direction based on a client need?

Here's a template you can use for outlining this step:

▸ Our first theme or value is:

▸ This, to us, means:

▸ We demonstrate this value to one another with these three behaviors:

3. Develop it. Identify areas that could help or hinder your value(s) or rules of engagement. These useful statements use flexibility as an example, but they can be adapted for whichever areas you decide to explore:

▸ These things could help our success in building a flexible, age-integrated culture, so we will start or continue them:

▸ These things could hinder our success in building a flexible, age-integrated culture, so we will stop them:

4. Defend it. Integrate your shared values and rules of engagement into the DNA of your team. Once the culture is set, then your connections have rich soil in which to flourish.

REFLECT:

▸ Have you ever felt judged for not complying with norms you didn't even know existed?

▸ Describe a time when you knew you belonged. Now share a time when you felt left out.

▸ Have you ever been in a healthy, diverse setting where everyone was welcome? What characteristics made that environment conducive for all?

ALL GENERATIONS AT THE TABLE

When I ask what has worked for companies in designing policies and a culture that works for people of all generations, the key point is always this: All generations must be engaged in the process. Also, it's a process.

When you bring all generations to the table together, on equal footing, for open discussion and free exchange of ideas, trust is built and everyone's perspective is broadened pretty quickly.

In a discussion of work ethic, you may learn that one generation defines it in terms of hours in the office while another defines it in terms of outcomes. How can you set policies that respect some workers' propensity to put in extra desk time at the office with equal regard for others' late-night work projects finished up at home?

Bring your team together and use Tony Moore's *Culture in 4D* model: dream it, design it, develop it, and defend it to set a clear definition of what "work ethic" means to your team and how you demonstrate it to one another.

In talking about compensation, you might learn that one generation really wants a good retirement plan, while another places more value on vacation time and work-related education. How can you give employees benefit options that maintain one generation's longstanding expectations while offering incentives that also draw in another generation's talent?

A conversation about technology could upend everything. The seemingly radical ideas raised by emerging generations – like replacing outdated systems or providing smartphones to create a platform for improved customer service – might give the bottom line a serious boost in the long run.

Cultivating a culture where all generations can thrive means recognizing the value that everyone has to contribute – and making sure everyone has a seat at the table and a voice that's heard.

CHAPTER 14

STEP 5: COACH
Develop a framework for feedback

THE UNLIKELY MENTOR

Fresh out of college, I was bright-eyed and ready to join the "real world." My dream at the time was to be a news reporter, so when I was offered a reporting job in one of my favorite cities, Colorado Springs, I could barely contain my excitement.

I'll never forget my first studio session with Terry, a 60-something journalist with an impressive work history. He was incredible on the air; his voice tracks would make your ears melt! Ready to show him my best, I put on my headphones, pulled my shoulders back, leaned into the mic, and read my script like a champ!

On the third sentence, Terry stopped me and started yelling about everything that was wrong with my voicing. I repeated a silent mantra to myself: "Don't cry. Don't cry. Don't cry." But trying not to cry only made it worse, and I wound up ugly crying on my first day. Who does that? I was embarrassed, and Terry felt horrible.

Clearly, he was frustrated with my performance on air, and he communicated that in a direct way. This makes sense; more than half of the men in Terry's generation are veterans, so naturally their communication style is based on the military chain of command.

I grew up in a generation with more positive, self-esteem-based communication. So, I didn't have the awareness that I wasn't good at broadcasting!

At the same time, I was frustrated with his aversion to using some of the newer technologies we relied on in the studio – things that, to me, were second nature.

It took a while to figure out which direction to go, but finally we struck a deal: I would help Terry learn the technology if he'd coach me on how to do better on the air. It wasn't an overnight fix, but it was a start, and we both worked at it.

He tried harder to deliver constructive criticism in a way that wouldn't make me want to run to a corner and bawl. I tried to develop a tougher skin and to talk him through the technology.

This positive change in our working relationship made a difference; before long, we had an amazing synergy that showed on the air. Having a great product – in this case a news show – only happened when we learned how to complement one another, allowing our strengths to shine while we worked together on our development areas.

Somewhere along the way, Terry started calling me "Princess Jess" for my once-sheltered ways, and I called him "Your Majesty" in lighthearted deference to his vast experience and knowledge. He turned out to be one of the best mentors I've ever had.

The Bottom Line: Sharing constructive feedback can be hard, especially across generations.

The Solution: Clarify your intent and expected behaviors, offer consistent two-way feedback, and be open to improving together through mentoring and reverse-mentoring.

1. CLARIFY YOUR INTENT

When giving feedback, it's important to communicate your intent. We often forget to do this part, and it can make a big difference in how the coaching is perceived.

Consider the Intent, Behavior, Results (IBR) model[49] to frame your message clearly:

INTENT: Why are you having the conversation or meeting?

Use 2–3 positive, directional sentences explaining why the conversation is happening.

BEHAVIOR: What action steps will you need to take?

Be clear what behaviors are expected. Behaviors are the visible things you do to jointly accomplish the intent.

RESULTS: How will you know when you're successful?

Make it measurable and specific to the work at hand. If the result matches your intent, celebrate! What's celebrated gets repeated. If the result doesn't match the intent, ask what went wrong in the behaviors.

Our brains are wired for negativity; it's a survival thing. In coaching, it's our job to guide others down positive paths by communicating a positive intent. Consider this example of two different approaches:

▸ Liz is called in for a meeting with her boss, who tells her, "I'm enrolling you in a public speaking course." She spends the rest of the day worrying because this must mean she's doing a terrible job in meetings and presentations.

▸ Alecia is called in for a meeting with her boss, who tells her, "I see a lot of potential in you, and I want to help your professional development, so I'm enrolling you in a public speaking course." She's thrilled at the opportunity and texts her mom to say how excited she is that her boss has taken notice of her potential.

The content of the message delivered to Liz and Alecia – that they've been signed up for a public speaking course – was the same. But the way it was delivered made a huge difference in how it was received.

When the positive intent was shared, the message was received positively; when no intent was shared, the message was received negatively. This is why sharing intent is so important: it clarifies the meaning behind the message.

The next step, after signing the employees up for the public speaking course, would be to communicate expected behaviors. For example, they're expected to attend a speaking course and practice each new speaking skill in a workplace setting.

If they're successful in following the expected steps and, in the process, make progress toward better public speaking, that should be celebrated! If not, the question is what went wrong in the behaviors. By focusing on the behaviors rather than the person, hard messages are much easier to receive.

2. GIVE CONTINUOUS FEEDBACK

When you're leading or supervising others, particularly if they're members of younger generations, it's also important to provide positive and constructive feedback about how they're doing.

Keep in mind that if they're young in their experiences, they may not be sure how to baseline their efforts – and if they're used to the constant feedback loop of social media, a lack of feedback from you may be viewed as a troubling silence.

Rather than waiting for a traditional once-a-year performance review, hold informal conversations as needed and consider setting up consistent check-in meetings to help them gauge their work and make improvements in real time.

3. BE OPEN TO RECEIVE FEEDBACK

If you are the person receiving the behavior-based feedback, what do you do if it is not so positive? Constructive coaching can be tough to swallow, especially if you're new on the job and enthusiastic to do well. But before dismissing the feedback as wrong, pause.

And then take a deep breath and consider what was shared with you: Could there be some truth to it? Evaluating feedback objectively, even when it stings, is a great opportunity for personal growth and development.

4. MENTOR AND REVERSE-MENTOR

More and more, the Millennial generation is involved in leading our organizations and institutions. Are you doing all you can to equip and empower them for success? Are you teaching them everything you've learned and sharing your wisdom forward?

If you have years of knowledge and experience, then you have the opportunity to make a difference in rising generations, one life at a time. Consider whose life you could be investing in.

At the same time, consider that mentoring is a two-way street. The phrase "reverse-mentoring" may have entered the corporate world in the 1990s, when General Electric's Jack Welch mandated that his top executives learn communication and e-business technology from younger employees. The concept, however, isn't new. It's simply the mindset that mentoring is mutually beneficial: an up, down, all-around exchange of knowledge across age, generation, and other boundaries.

I've seen CEOs learn how to tweet from 19-year old interns and leaders strengthen their strategies because of deep questions posed by their group members. To approach mentoring as a mutually beneficial process can help you to re-frame it as a useful two-way exchange.

5. IT'S OK NOT TO HAVE ALL THE ANSWERS

Remember that with all generations mentoring is built on relationships and trust, both of which take time to build. Mentoring is not about having all the answers or following a specific program; it's about caring, listening, asking questions, checking in, sharing your experiences, and helping the person you're mentoring to be successful.

Mentoring can be as simple as meeting for coffee or even checking in with a text. My mentor and I both love power walking, so when we need to catch up, we hit the trail and talk it up!

TRY THIS TOOL: MUTUALLY BENEFICIAL MENTORING

In the past, mentoring and coaching were typically considered a one-way conversation or the gaining of experience from someone older. But, as every good mentor knows, it's really a two-way exchange, and we can learn from those who are younger than us, too.

If you're interested in mutually beneficial mentoring or coaching but don't know how to structure it, consider this framework developed by Ken Blanchard and Clair Diaz-Ortiz:

▸ **M**ission: Create a clear purpose statement for the mentoring relationship. Why are you together as mentor and mentee, and what do you hope to get out of it?

▸ **E**ngagement: Establish how and when you'll engage with each other and figure out what those meetings will look like.

▸ **N**etworking: Discuss how you might expand each other's horizons in life and work.

▸ **T**rust: Take time to build a culture of trust in your mentoring relationship.

▸ **O**pportunities: Ask what new opportunities you might create for each other.

▸ **R**eview and Renewal: Periodically check in with each other to see how your relationship aligns with the mission you set out and make sure it's still a good fit as you both grow and change over time.[50]

Here are some mentoring and reverse-mentoring questions to get you started:

In life:

▸ When you look back on your life one day, what do you want to see?

▸ What does success – or a life well-lived – look like to you?

▸ What's the most significant life lesson you've learned so far?

▸ How would you describe the season of life you're in now?

▸ What do you hope for your future?

In work:

▸ What was your first job?

▸ How did you decide on your career?

▸ What is the greatest lesson you have learned on the job?

▸ What is one skill you can teach me?

▸ What is one skill you'd like to learn from me?

REFLECT:

▸ Who has been a coach or mentor of influence in your life? What qualities made them so impactful?

▸ Please share an example of a time you were given constructive feedback. How was it communicated to you? How did you receive it?

▸ How can you use Intent, Behavior, Results (IBR) to clear up the communication lines?

LEARN FROM EACH OTHER

Coaching, mentoring, and reverse-mentoring is the glue that bind generations together.

Whether you're a senior leader learning how to use Slack from your new hire or a 20-something learning the ropes of business from your 50-something friend, it's the continuous loop of feedback that helps us improve from generation to generation.

CHAPTER 15

STEP 6: ADAPT

Apply a generational lens to forecast the future

OH, SNAP

Snapchat. Oh, Snapchat. Nothing in me wanted to try the social media application. I didn't understand the purpose or find the interface intuitive or user-friendly. Half the time, I didn't know if I was snapping or chatting.

It was during speaking prep that I uncovered how popular the app is among my younger Gen Z friends. Couldn't they just hang onto Instagram? I like it so much better!

With a bit of a negative attitude, I decided I should practice what I preach: understanding my audience and meeting them where they are.

I didn't learn very well on my own, so I engaged the help of one of my favorite college students, Nelson. Within 30 minutes he taught me why and how his friends use Snapchat, and then he helped me practice snapping. Is that what it's called?

A strange thing happened after I learned more about the tool — I kind of liked it! The concept of capturing moments as they happen and then quickly letting them go is not only efficient, but a refreshing approach to communication – and life.

The Bottom Line: The world is rapidly changing. Keeping up can feel intimidating and overwhelming.

The Solution: Partner with different generations to understand and lean in to change, combining your perspectives to create a thriving future.

CHANGE RISES

Why did I feel the need to hold onto all of my pictures and moments? Snapchat inspired me to ask deeper questions. Adopting the younger generation's communication method helped me to learn and grow – and reset my relationship with change in multiple areas of life.

From learning how to selfie without a double chin to being present as moments come and go, I've picked up all sorts of new skills simply by letting the next generation teach me things outside my comfort zone!

One of my favorite things about studying generational trends is the anticipatory lens it provides us to forecast where things might be going. Among the factors that will impact how it looks in the future:

the aging workforce, increasing diversity, and new developments in technology.

Rising generations especially give us clues about how the workplace landscape will shift with it. Particularly as Millennials and Gen Z grow in influence, trends like a growing emphasis on self-development, remote working, freelance roles, and future-proofing strategies are expected.[51]

We usually can't predict what will change – often the biggest changes are the least expected – but looking through a generational lens can help us to prepare for what's coming in the future. This is a good practice.

TRY THIS TOOL: THE WORKPLACE OF 2030

One way of thinking about the future is through an exercise like this: Visualize, in specific terms, how things might change over the next decade or so. Using what you've learned about generational trends, please answer these questions about the workplace of the future:

 The news headline for the workplace of 2030 is:

 The supporting hashtag will be:

▌ To prepare for the workplace of 2030:

  ▸ What should our organization start doing?

  ▸ What should our organization stop doing?

  ▸ What should our organization continue doing?

Now for the really hard question. What do you want your personal headline of 2030 to say? These questions can help you to figure it out:

📄 My headline of 2030 is:

 My supporting hashtag will be:

▌ To prepare for the future I envision:

  ▸ What should I start doing?

  ▸ What should I stop doing?

  ▸ What should I continue doing?

REFLECT:

▸ Have you ever been resistant to a change, but then ended up liking it?

▸ What's the biggest change you've witnessed in the workplace so far?

▸ What's the biggest change you think will impact the workplace of the future?

GROW AS YOU GO

As Dr. Henry Cloud said in *Necessary Endings*, moving forward to the next level always requires leaving something behind, and that isn't always easy.[52]

Have you ever worked really hard for something that ultimately didn't work out? Maybe you've loved and lost. Maybe you've tried and failed. I've experienced all of the above – and even though the endings always pivoted me to better places, it sure was painful in the process of accepting and letting go.

We must honor the tension that sits in the middle of a generational shift: that new beginnings are directly linked with endings.

On one hand, it's a very exciting time for new and innovative ideas. Possibilities abound as we empower emerging generations and they lead us into the future.

On the other hand, it's incredibly difficult to let go – not only of what's comfortable, but of what were once new ideas that have since run their course. Things people were really excited about and worked hard to build.

Honoring individual and organizational stories and experiences is critical in the midst of change. Here are some ways that companies navigate it:

▸ **Make Grief Good.** As we learn about generational trends, change is a natural by-product. We have to grieve what was before we can accept what is and will be. For example, I infuse Elisabeth Kübler-Ross's grief model into trainings in experiential ways like a balloon release.

▸ **Let it Go Together.** Moe Girkins, a former AT&T executive, had to oversee the shutting down of one of their businesses, so they had a funeral – a real ceremony to say good-bye:

"We got everyone together and told stories, reminisced, and cried. We celebrated the past and said good-bye to it. And we buried a time capsule. We told everyone to put something in the time capsule and told them that we would bury it on the site. The building was going away, and we wanted them to feel that although the business was ending, we would celebrate what they had all done over the years and preserve it for the future. It was really healthy, and it allowed them to say good-bye, leave it behind, and move on to the next stage."[53]

▸ **Re- Imagine Together.** Host a visioning day for the future you hope to attain. Using the "Headline of the Future" exercise is a great way to do it.

▸ **Communicate the New Vision Often.** Engage both head and heart as you clarify the vision over and over, while modeling behaviors for others. Involve people at all levels, inviting them to help shape the future and integrate the familiar with the new. For those who are open to change – inspire them. For those who are resistant to change – remind them how the pain of staying the same would be worse than the pain of changing. Continuously assess how the change is going and keep a clear feedback loop of communication. Adapt and improve accordingly.

What's one way your company can honor the people, stories, and memories of the past, memorializing what was while making space for the great future that will be?

The reality is that no matter which generation you belong to – whether Traditionalists who'd still rather work at a desk without a computer or Millennials who are no longer on the leading edge from a smartphone perspective – things are going to keep on changing. Even Gen Z will one day find themselves shaking their heads at whatever new thing is coming down the pike and wondering whether it will be of any use.

To thrive amid rapid change, we must not sit back and decry the departure from the way things used to be, but rather take time to understand the trends, look within, and adapt our styles and strategies accordingly. This doesn't mean we compromise our core values or convictions; it simply suggests that we discern our times and position ourselves, companies, and causes in relevant ways.

New positioning starts with a mindset shift, which is good news because that's within our influence. Research shows our thoughts tell our brain what to do, meaning our thinking patterns are not fixed but can change. This is called a growth mindset, and it's critical for success.

CHAPTER 16

STEP 7: SHARE
Develop a process to transfer knowledge

PART TEACHER, PART STUDENT

I spent a day with a large foundation that was trying to integrate the next generation into their board pipeline; in an effort to do this, they started a youth board.

It was a good idea in theory, but the established leaders and the new youth board members didn't know how to act around each other in meetings. And so we hosted a board retreat where they could learn how to speak the same language and then use their diverse perspectives and skill sets to teach each other.

After learning next-generation communication preferences, experienced board members taught financial perpetuity – an important aspect of success – to the youth board in ways they could understand.

Then, the youth board suggested the two most important social media channels for the foundation to embed in its strategy to engage their peers in the foundation's mission and legacy. And they taught the experienced board how to use these tools, doing so while using their new strategies to communicate with their elders.

Together, they determined how the full and youth board could come together in productive ways.

By the time I left, they were talking organically in age-mixed groups and having dinner together. They're now supporting one another in life, business, and high school sports. By being part teacher and part student, everyone felt they were on equal footing to help each other and the foundation to thrive.

The Bottom Line: Knowledge exchange doesn't just happen. It has to be cultivated.

The Solution: Create a formal process to identify, capture, and share knowledge from generation to generation. This helps ensure personal and institutional legacy.

KNOWLEDGE TRANSFER IS INTENTIONAL

In most companies I work with, knowledge-hoarding is a problem – particularly among seasoned leaders. Knowledge hoarding is keeping experience-based, business critical knowledge – what *Harvard Business Review* writer Dorothy Leonard calls "deep smarts" – to oneself.

"By definition, those deep smarts are still valuable to the organization and underlie future as well as current success,"

Leonard writes. "They may be technical, but they can also be managerial, as when an experienced manager has hard-earned skills in problem identification and solution, crucial relationships with customers, or a detailed understanding of how to innovate."[54]

"Baby Boomer brain drain" is another term many use to describe what happens when critical knowledge walks out the company door as people retire, without being captured by others within the organization. This can be a major risk for companies.

According to the Leonard, knowledge-hoarding happens for three reasons: Lack of financial incentives, personal ego, and discontent with a company.[55] While all three of these can be hard to address, it is possible. Here are some steps to get you started:

1. CREATE A CULTURE OF SHARING

Embed knowledge-sharing as a core value in your culture. Put an emphasis on mentoring, transferring knowledge, and leaving a legacy. Research shows those who've been mentored are a lot more likely to mentor. Here are some examples:

▸ *Forbes Magazine* launched an "at 25" series sharing what today's successful entrepreneurs were doing and thinking at 25. Some were stacking silverware in a serving job; others were beginning to capture their ideas. One thing they were all doing, however, was learning valuable lessons that prepared them for the future. The series humanized top innovators, making them relatable to everyone and giving them a platform to share their lessons learned. Could your leaders do something like this?

▸ A company used an internal network to host a lunch-and-learn series featuring "one thing you want to teach and one thing you want to learn." So many talents outside the employees' job roles were discovered that the company developed a team of internal consultants to solve challenges within. Not only was the program a big hit with employees, but it generated direct benefits to the company!

▸ A nonprofit launched "next generation shadowing and sharing days" where young new hires buddied up with more experienced workers. They went to lunch with them, attended meetings together, and then had to report what they had learned and teach someone else.

2. FORMALIZE KNOWLEDGE SHARING BY PRIORITIZING, CAPTURING, AND TRAINING

First, identify and prioritize what type or types of knowledge need to be captured and what roles are critical for your short- and long-term strategy.

Explicit knowledge is knowledge that can be easily captured, articulated, and shared from person to person. For example: a "how-to" manual, written procedures, or videos on how to use a product.

Tacit knowledge is knowledge gained from personal experience, which is hard to teach simply by writing it down – for example: riding a bike, playing the piano, driving a car. In the workplace things like social skills, the ability to read people, and intuition are examples of tacit knowledge that's important, yet difficult to pass along.

Second, clarify who owns knowledge transfer – who supports it and ensures it's accurate. Make it clear how knowledge is captured and where and when it's shared.

You can then capture knowledge via documents (think checklists, templates, playbooks), technology (wikis, blogs, shared sites), and human sharing (education, interviews, mentoring and reverse-mentoring, storytelling, conferences, etc.).

Finally, help different ages and stages speak the same language so they can share knowledge and experiences, and train to multiple learning and communication styles. Learning leaders report work shadowing and coaching as the most prevalent practices used for knowledge transfer.[56]

3. INCENTIVIZE TALENT DEVELOPMENT

Reward knowledge-sharing. For example, within some companies, employees cannot be promoted until they can show they've mentored a successor. Other companies have a whole compensation model called gain sharing, which is rooted in how a team accomplishes a common goal. The purpose is to keep everyone aligned and accountable for success.

TRY THIS TOOL: YOUR KNOWLEDGE-SHARING PLAN

Create a knowledge-sharing plan by addressing these questions:

▸ What type of knowledge do you need to share?

☐ Explicit knowledge: routine parts of my job, step-by-step checklists, etc.

☐ Tacit (intuitive) knowledge: what I know from experience

☐ Explicit and tacit knowledge

▸ Who needs to know what you do to be successful?

- How can you capture your knowledge so it will endure throughout the years?

  - ☐ Documents (checklists, templates, playbooks)

  - ☐ Technology (wikis, blogs, videos, shared sites)

  - ☐ Human sharing (education, interviews, mentoring and reverse-mentoring, storytelling, coaching, job shadowing, conferences, etc.)

- Who can check to make sure your knowledge is accurate?

- When should you share it with the recipients?

- Do you need training to share knowledge?

- What's your next step to share what you've learned?

REFLECT:

- Who shared knowledge with you?

- Have you thanked them lately?

- What are some ways you can pay it forward?

EMPTY YOUR CUP

I attended a conference where pastor and leadership guru Andy Stanley offered a challenge to the audience. "Empty your cup," he said. "Share what you've experienced to help others."

He said that sharing knowledge is less about filling up someone else's cup because, even with the best intent and imagination, we can never fully understand what another person needs. On the other hand, we do know what we've learned and can healthfully and wisely share it.

Andy's talk impacted me on a deep level, and before I knew it "empty your cup" became the vision for my life. My personal mission statement – "to live fully, learn deeply, and share to help others" – is rooted out of it. It's changed the way I live life and run my business.

What have you learned in life that you can share to empty your cup? Who needs to hear it?

Don't store up your knowledge, wisdom, and experiences. Share them to help others who show themselves worthy of receiving. Live with succession in mind. Find a mentor. Be a mentor. It's through the pouring out that everyone fills up!

CHAPTER 17

TEACH ME YOUR DANCE

A summary of how to get different generations in sync

In a recent research project, my partners and I put intergenerational teams in a room and gave them a problem to solve. Watching them interact was a lot like being at a middle school dance. Do you remember those days?

Different groups (in this case generations) stood on different sides of the room. It seemed like they wanted to dance but didn't know how. Do they ask a partner? Or wait to be asked?

When they tried to "dance," it looked as if one was doing the foxtrot and another the floss, one the waltz and another the nae nae. By nature, they didn't jive.

It was awkward. And totally normal!

Coming together across generations is not easy at first. It takes practice, patience, trust, and hard work. But then you get in a groove, and it's a sight to see!

KEY TAKEAWAYS FROM PART II

Remember these seven steps as you enter the generational dance:

▸ **Understand:** The first and foundational step of bridging generational gaps is to help different generations get to know one another and learn how to "speak a common language."

▸ **Appreciate:** When you encounter what you think might be a generational conflict, pause and get your mind steady. Filter check by assessing whether there's anything in your personal lens hindering you from seeing others in an accurate light. Step back and take perspective, considering alternate points of view. Then, adapt by bringing your diverse viewpoints together for breakthrough new realities.

▸ **Communicate:** When communicating with different generations, ask their preferred channel and style rather than assuming. Bring together an intergenerational team to figure out how to best keep in touch on a team level. Use story to connect across generations; research shows this time-tested method unites the brains of the storyteller and listener, breaking down potential barriers to pure communication.

▸ **Cultivate:** Always clarify expectations as a team to ensure alignment. For example, what does "efficient" mean to your team? Make sure to define it and then list supporting behaviors that are commonly used on the job. For example, "To us, efficiency means returning emails within 48 hours."

▸ **Coach:** When communicating and coaching across generations, remember IBR: Intent, Behavior, Results. Whether you're leading a meeting or offering feedback, these three steps can help you keep things clear.

▸ **Adapt:** Generations have often been looked at in the rearview mirror, but they're also a way to see where things may be going. Change evokes a range of emotions; honor the tension, using it to propel you forward. Memorializing milestone and making strong plans for the future – while including all people – is a great way to prepare now for what's next.

▸ **Share:** Knowledge transfer is one of the most important, yet least utilized, opportunities for personal and organizational legacy and success. Prioritize the knowledge that needs to be captured, formalize the process for capturing and storing it, and train people on how to do it. Mentoring and reverse-mentoring – where everyone learns from each other – is the glue.

My friend Ron Harris once told me diversity means you're inviting different generations to your dance. Inclusion means you're asking them to dance. Cultural competency is letting your friend from a different generation choose the music.

May we all enter the generational dance with a posture of humility, seeking first to learn the tunes and moves of others.

REFLECT:

▸ What is one thing you see differently after reading Part II?

▸ How will you apply what you've learned?

▸ Assess yourself. Based on your answers below, what's one thing you can do to connect across generations?

👍	👎	
☐	☐	I am a champion of generational diversity.
☐	☐	I pause when generational friction occurs.
☐	☐	I have evaluated my paradigm, or lens, for seeing the world.
☐	☐	I have taken time to consider other points of view.
☐	☐	I am willing to combine perspectives to create better outcomes.
☐	☐	I ask different generations what communication channels work best for them.
☐	☐	I meet different generations "where they are."
☐	☐	I am open for feedback from those older and younger than me.
☐	☐	I am open for change.
☐	☐	I am a mentor.
☐	☐	I have a mentor.
☐	☐	I am sharing my knowledge, wisdom, and experiences.
☐	☐	I am doing all I can to leave a strong legacy.

MOVE FROM INSIGHTS TO ACTION:

▸ Intentionally connect with someone from a different generation. Have lunch together or work together on a project and see what you can learn and create together.

▸ List three bold moves you can take to apply what you've learned in this book.

CHAPTER 18

REGENERATE

A challenge to learn from and improve with each generation

"All good men and women must take responsibility to create legacies that will take the next generation to a level we could only imagine." —Jim Rohn

THE FLIGHT ATTENDANT

I watched as a young flight attendant welcomed passengers on board a recent flight. It was her first time making announcements, and she was filled with excitement – and nervousness.

As her trembling hands completed the last click of the seatbelt demonstration, she looked up as if to gauge feedback on her performance. And that's when it happened: a chorus of claps, cheers, and high fives from passengers.

It was a moment of pure joy for her – and for us!

We've all had "firsts" in life. First classes. First dates. First jobs. New experiences that feel invigorating, scary, and everything in between. And, most likely, we've all had people who cheered us along.

In the busyness of life, it's easy to miss the miracles of these moments. We've got to be intentional about asking: Are we taking time to see and clap for those who are rising up?

Who is someone you see potential in? Is there a person you feel led to mentor, invest in, or affirm? As emerging generations seek their fit in life and work, how can you help?

Encourage a young friend by writing their name in this image, taking a picture, and posting on social media or texting them to express awesome qualities you see in them! If you share on social media, make sure to hashtag #ReGenerate so we can celebrate the next generation.

A CHALLENGE TO EMERGING GENERATIONS

To the generations who are rising up to make a mark on our world: you're doing great! I believe in you and can't wait to see how your story unfolds! I encourage you to connect with those who've gone before you. Ask about their stories and experiences. Honor them by listening to what they say and implementing the wisdom they teach.

Be open to and respectful of advice from established generations and build on that knowledge to make improvements as you work to make yourselves worthy leaders. Be willing to show respect for other experiences and listen well as you work to make this a better world for future generations; someday, you too will be passing the torch.

THANK THOSE WHO'VE CHEERED YOU ON

A Starbucks gift card and a letter: "I love your passion for generations. I encourage you to grab a coffee and commit one night a week to better understand what it is and how it helps others."

Miles of walking and talking to process life. Discussions around the kitchen table and around my desk at work. Notes that show up in my mailbox. "I've been where you are, and I understand how you feel. You will fly again. I promise."

New faces of support that emerge when I least expected it. "You are doing well." "How can I help?" "Here's what I've learned." "Great things are ahead." "My door is always open." "You belong."

When I think back on my journey, these are some of the moments when elders in my life have stepped in without even being asked – to listen, love and advise. Today, many of them sit on my personal and professional boards of directors.

My heart overflows with gratitude for those who are a few steps ahead in life and take time to share their wisdom and encouragement with me. What a gift!

Who has done that for you? Who has given you a start, believed in you, and invested in your life just because they genuinely care? Who was cheering you on in your "junior flight attendant" first? Have you thanked them lately?

Honor them by writing their name in this image, taking a picture, and posting on social media or texting them to express the awesome qualities you see in them! If you share on social media, make sure to hashtag #ReGenerate so we can celebrate our elders who've paved the way.

A CHALLENGE TO ESTABLISHED GENERATIONS

Thank you for the solid foundation you've laid and the knowledge you've accumulated over many years of experience. The roots of your legacy run deep.

Be intentional about passing · along life lessons, traditions, knowledge, and wisdom to emerging generations – and make an effort to communicate these ideas in a way they'll understand. Whether or not they seem ready to listen, they need your knowledge and mentoring. Empower them to learn, value what they bring to the table, and live with succession in mind, preparing to help them take the reins of leadership when you're ready to step down.

REGENERATE

Right now we sit at a crossroads of challenge, change, and opportunity to thrive. The choices that we make now will echo in our culture for decades.

One of the great commonalities, true to all generations, is that in a tumultuous period of intense social change, we all need each other and can learn from one another.

No matter which generation you're part of, remember that sharing stories and experiences strengthens our connections and our understanding of both past and present realities in shaping who we are as people and organizations.

Though there's always potential for misunderstanding and conflict when different generations interact, there's also potential to work together in ways that result in a better outcome than any one generation could achieve on its own.

So, let's listen to and help one another and put in the effort necessary to make our generational differences and strengths work together for a thriving future.

Experience has proven that companies, schools, churches, families, and communities that leverage the collective strengths of all generations will thrive time after time: they will ReGenerate.

EXPLORE MORE

Thank you for reading *ReGenerate*!

To learn more about connecting generations, visit re-generations.org.

If you like what you find, stay in touch on Twitter and Instagram (@ReGenerations), Facebook (ReGenerations), or YouTube (ReGensVideos). Our hashtag is #ReGenerate.

Email info@re-generations.org to sign up for ongoing content, or to book a speaking or training event for your organization, cause, or conference.

Now, let's #ReGenerate!

REFERENCES

1.   David Livemore, *Driven by Difference* (New York: AMACOM, 2016), 10.

2.   "The Great Generational Divide: New Study Shows Unaddressed Resentment Between Baby Boomers, Gen X and Millennials Saps Productivity by as Much as 12%," VitalSmarts, February 5, 2014, https://www.vitalsmarts.com/press/2014/02/the-great-generational-divide-new-study-shows-unaddressed-resentment-between-baby-boomers-gen-x-and-millennials-saps-productivity-by-as-much-as-12/.

3.   Amy Adkins, "Millennials: The Job-Hopping Generation," Gallup Workplace, May 16, 2016, https://www.gallup.com/workplace/236474/millennials-job-hopping-generation.aspx.

4.   Dan Bursch, "Managing the Multi-Generational Workplace," Kenan-Flagler Business School, 2014, https://www.kenan-flagler.unc.edu/~/media/Files/documents/executive-development/managing-the-multigenerational-workplace-white-paper.pdf.

5.   Karl Mannheim, "The Problem of Generations," in *From Karl Mannheim*, ed. Kurt H. Wolff, 2nd expanded edition (New Brunswick: Transaction, 1993), 365.

6.   William Strauss and Neil Howe, *Generations: The History of America's Future, 1584 to 2069* (New York: Morrow, 1991).

7.   Tammy Erickson and Timothy Blevins, "Generations & Geography: Overview," Moxie Insight, May 26, 2011, https://www.slideshare.net/MoxieInsight/generations-and-geography-white-paper.

8.   "Millennials: Confident. Connected. Open to Change," Pew Research Center, accessed January 19, 2015, https://www.pewresearch.org/wp-content/uploads/sites/3/2010/10/millennials-confident-connected-open-to-change.pdf.

9.   Barna Group OmniPoll. Study conducted in 2014 with a representative sample of at least 1,000 U.S. adults, ages 18+. Data was conducted by telephone (including with cellphone users) and online.

10. Anya Kamenetz, "The Four-Year Career," *Fast Company* (January 12, 2012).

11. "Median Household Income in the United States," DaveManuel.com, accessed January 19, 2015. https://www.davemanuel.com/median-household-income.php.

12. Les Christie, "America's Homes Are Bigger than Ever," CNNMoney, accessed January 19, 2015, http://money.cnn.com/2014/06/04/real_estate/american-home-size/.

13. Mitra Toossi and Elka Torpey, "Older workers: Labor Force Trends and Career Options." U.S. Bureau of Labor Statistics, May 2017, https://www.bls.gov/careeroutlook/2017/article/older-workers.htm.

14. "Births, Deaths, Marriages, and Divorces," *Statistical Abstract of the United States*, U.S. Census Bureau, accessed January 19, 2015, http://www.census.gov/prod/2011pubs/11statab/vitstat.pdf.

15. Stephanie Neal, "Generation X-Change: Don't Underestimate the Power Influence of Gen X Leaders," DDI Global Leadership Forecast 2018, https://www.ddiworld.com/glf2018/generation-x-leaders; Development Dimensions International Inc., The Conference Board Inc., EYGM Limited, 2018.

16. Sylvia Ann Hewlett, "4 Ways to Retain Gen Xers," *Harvard Business Review* (September 4, 2014).

17. Sylvia Ann Hewlett and Lauren Chivee, *The X Factor Tapping into the Strengths of the 35- to 48-Year-Old Generation* (New York: Rare Bird, 2013).

18. Jonathan Vespa, "The Changing Economics and Demographics of Young Adulthood: 1975–2016," U.S. Census Bureau, April 2017, https://www.census.gov/content/dam/Census/library/publications /2017/demo/p20-579.pdf.

19. "The PreparedU Project's Report on Millennial Minds," *The Millennial Mind Goes to Work*, Bentley University, accessed January 19, 2015, http://www.bentley.edu/newsroom/latest-headlines/mind-of-millennial.

20. Richard Fry, "Millennials Projected to Overtake Baby Boomers as America's Largest Generation," Pew Research Center, March 1, 2018, https://www.pewresearch.org/fact-tank/2018/03/01/millennials-overtake-baby-boomers/.

21. Richard Fry, "Millennials are the Largest Generation in the U.S. Labor Force," Pew Research Center, April 11, 2018 https://www.pewresearch.org/fact-tank/2018/04/11/millennials-largest-generation-us-labor-force/.

22. "Social Networking Fact Sheet," Pew Research Center, accessed January 19, 2015. http://www.pewinternet.org/fact-sheets/social-networking-fact-sheet/.

23. "Millennials in Adulthood," Pew Research Center, accessed January 19, 2015, http://www.pewsocialtrends.org/2014/03/07/millennials-in-adulthood/.

24. "Atheism Doubles Among Generation Z," Barna Group, January 24, 2018, https://www.barna.com/research/atheism-doubles-among-generation-z/.

25. Susannah Fox and Lee Rainie, "The Web at 25 in the U.S. Part 1: How the Internet has Woven Itself into American Life," Pew Research Center, February 27, 2014, https://www.pewinternet.org/2014/02/27/part-1-how-the-internet-has-woven-itself-into-american-life/.

26. Joeri Van den Bergh, "Millennials vs. Gen Z," Cable & Telecommunications Association for Marketing, 2016, https://www.ctam.com/strategic-collaboration/Pages/Millennials-vs--Gen-Z.aspx.

27. David Stillman and Jonah Stillman, *GenZ @ Work: How the Next Generation is Transforming the Workplace* (New York: Harper Business, 2017), 198.

28. Ibid., 164, 158, 165.

29. Richard Fry and Kim Parker, "Early Benchmarks Show 'Post-Millennials' On Track to Be Most Diverse, Best-Educated Generation Yet," Pew Research Center, November 15, 2018, https://www.pewsocialtrends.org/2018/11/15/early-benchmarks-show-post-millennials-on-track-to-be-most-diverse-best-educated-generation-yet/.

30. Stillman and Stillman, *GenZ @ Work*, 108.

31. Kim Parker, Nikki Graf, and Ruth Igielnik, "Generation Z Looks a Lot Like Millennials on Key Social and Political Issues," Pew Research Center, January 17, 2019, https://www.pewsocialtrends.org/2019/01/17/generation-z-looks-a-lot-like-millennials-on-key-social-and-political-issues/.

32. "Looking Further with Ford: 2015 Trends," Ford Motor Company, Accessed on March 3, 2019, https://www.at.ford.com/content/dam/atford/archive/2014_NA/Dec/Ford-2015-TrendReportBook.pdf.

33. Lizzy Gurdus, "Your World Changed Forever in 2007, Get With the Program, Thomas Friedman Says," CNBC, November 22, 2016, https://www.cnbc.com/2016/11/22/your-world-changed-forever-in-2007-with-iphone-and-tech-boom-thomas-friedman.html.

34. "2016 National Survey on Drug Use and Health," Substance Abuse and Mental Health Services Administration, accessed on

February 25, 2019,

https://www.samhsa.gov/data/sites/default/files/NSDUH-

DetTabs-2016/NSDUH-DetTabs-2016.pdf.

35. Jean M. Twenge, *iGen: Why Today's Super-Connected Kids are Growing Up Less Rebellious, More Tolerant, Less Happy – and Completely Unprepared for Adulthood – and What That Means for the Rest of Us* (New York: Atria Books, 2017), 93.

36. Fry and Parker, "Early Benchmarks Show 'Post-Millennials" On Track to Be Most Diverse, Best-Educated Generation Yet."

37. Stillman and Stillman, *GenZ @ Work*, 165.

38. Twenge, *iGen*, 93.

39. "What You Need To Know About Gen Z," Autotrader and Kelly Blue Book 2016, https://b2b.autotrader.com/agame/pdf/2016-gen-z-study-autotrader-kbb.pdf.

40. Stephen R. Covey, *Seven Habits of Highly Effective People: Restoring the Character Ethic* (New York: Free Press, 2004), 235.

41. Richard Fry, Ruth Igielnik, and Eileen Patten, "How Millennials Today Compare with Their Grandparents 50 Years Ago," Pew Research Center, March 16, 2018, https://www.pewresearch.org/fact-tank/2018/03/16/how-millennials-compare-with-their-grandparents/.

42. "The Five Whys: Understanding the Root Cause of a Problem,"
Six Sigma, February 22, 2017, https://www.6sigma.us/it/five-whys-
root-cause-analysis/.

43. Livemore, *Driven by Difference*, 236.

44. "Generations Have a Lot in Common, Too," Kenan-Flagler
Business School Executive Development Blog, February 9, 2017,
http://execdev.kenan-flagler.unc.edu/blog/generations-have-a-lot-
in-common-too.

45. John Scorza, "Millennials Usher in New Social Paradigm,"
Society for Human Resource Management, June 25, 2012,
https://www.shrm.org/hr-today/news/hr-
news/pages/millennialsusherinnewsocialparadigm.aspx.

46. Stephen R. Covey. *The 3rd Alternative: Solving Life's Most
Difficult Problems (*New York: Free Press, 2012), 9.

47. Ibid., 8-15.

48. Tony Moore, *Culture in 4D: The Blueprint for a Culture of
Engagement, Ownership, and Bottom-Line Performance*
(Lexington, Kentucky: Richter Publishing, 2018), 35, 36, 67, 85.

49. Copyright Staub Leadership, 2016. Used by ReGenerations
with permission.

50. "Ken Blanchard and Claire Diaz-Ortiz—How to Create a Mutually Beneficial Mentoring Relationship," Building a StoryBrand Podcast, https://podtail.com/podcast/building-a-story-brand-with-donald-miller-cla/50-ken-blanchard-and-claire-diaz-ortiz-how-to/.

51. Karen Gilchrist, "How Millennials and Gen Z are Reshaping the Future of the Workforce," CNBC, March 5, 2019, https://www.cnbc.com/2019/03/05/how-millennials-and-gen-z-are-reshaping-the-future-of-the-workforce.html.

52. Henry Cloud, *Necessary Endings: The Employees, Businesses, and Relationships That All of Us Have to Give Up in Order to Move Forward* (New York: Harper Business, 2010), 7.

53. Ibid., 211-212.

54. Dorothy Leonard, "How to Prevent Experts from Hoarding Knowledge," *Harvard Business Review*, December 18, 2014, https://hbr.org/2014/12/how-to-prevent-experts-from-hoarding-knowledge.

55. Ibid.

56. "Onboarding and Knowledge Transfer," Raytheon, 2012, https://trainingindustry.com/content/uploads/2017/07/onboarding-and-knowledge-transfer-report.pdf.

ACKNOWLEDGEMENTS

Thank you to Debra McCown Thomas for helping me translate the many words from my head and heart into the pages of this succinct book. I'm grateful for your edits, and I know the readers are, too! Most of all, I appreciate your friendship. I'm proud of what we've created together.

Thank you to René Rodgers for copy editing. I rest well at night knowing your wise eyes have reviewed my words. Thanks for the gift you bring to the table, and to my life.

Thank you to Matt Haynes and Briana Morris Fillers for the collaborative book cover design. You created a look that embodies the beauty of generational diversity, and – with the back-and-forth arrows – remind us to honor the past and the future and to continuously improve together.

Thank you to Briana Morris Fillers for designing the book art and graphics. Your touch on this work – and all my business communications – brings the message alive! I'm so thankful that you came into my professional life through your gift of design and are now one of my best friends.

Thank you to my clients, who continue to encourage and inspire me. Thank you for letting me into your world and sharing your stories with me. You teach me so much! Thanks, also, for letting me be me – better together flags, confetti pops, and all! One of the greatest honors of my life is when I get up to speak and you introduce me as your friend.

To the ReGenerator tribe, thanks for joining the movement to connect generations and share knowledge to improve our relationships, workplace, and world!

Thank you to David Golden, my mentor and friend. The day I met you was a game-changer. Thank you for seeing potential in me and for helping to bring it out. Thank you for always seeing ahead of where I am and for never giving me answers, but instead giving me questions to explore and books to read. You have been a gracious guide. I promise to share all you've taught me to help others.

Thank you to CeeGee McCord for being my friend, advocate, and teacher. Thank you for hosting my first learning series with your team, where much of the content in this book was born. You played a critical role in my start, and I will always be grateful for you.

Thank you to Tony Moore, my speaking partner and friend. I will forever be grateful we connected at Big Bend SHRM. Thank you for monthly calls to share what we're learning and where we continuously support and encourage one another. A highlight of my career was speaking on the same stage with you! And cheers to Aundra Moore, who has also become a sound advisor and friend.

Thank you to my awesome business manager, Katie Morgan. You are a gift from above. Thank you for listening, supporting, encouraging and cheering on this mission and message. Having you by my side has made this journey even more fun. I believe the best is yet to come.

Thank you to my tribe of besties: Sarah Jane, Carrie, Rachelle, Meredith, Carrico, Ryiah, and Amber. Thank you for doing life with me. Your friendship is a treasure.

Most of all, thank you to my family – Mom and Dad, Emily, Chris, Lilly Grace, Allie-Kate, Jason, and Holston Davis. You've been on this journey with me for a decade. Thank you for "getting it" and for always encouraging me to boldly live out this calling – like a horse with blinders on, as mom says. You are my world, and I love each of you deeply.